Cambridge Elements ≡

Elements in Shakespeare and Pedagogy
edited by
Liam E. Semler
University of Sydney
Gillian Woods
Birkbeck College, University of London

TEACHING WITH INTERACTIVE SHAKESPEARE EDITIONS

Laura B. Turchi
Arizona State University

CAMBRIDGE
UNIVERSITY PRESS

CAMBRIDGE
UNIVERSITY PRESS

Shaftesbury Road, Cambridge CB2 8EA, United Kingdom

One Liberty Plaza, 20th Floor, New York, NY 10006, USA

477 Williamstown Road, Port Melbourne, VIC 3207, Australia

314–321, 3rd Floor, Plot 3, Splendor Forum, Jasola District Centre, New Delhi – 110025, India

103 Penang Road, #05–06/07, Visioncrest Commercial, Singapore 238467

Cambridge University Press is part of Cambridge University Press & Assessment, a department of the University of Cambridge.

We share the University's mission to contribute to society through the pursuit of education, learning and research at the highest international levels of excellence.

www.cambridge.org
Information on this title: www.cambridge.org/9781009010924

DOI: 10.1017/9781009024105

First published 2023

A catalogue record for this publication is available from the British Library.

ISBN 978-1-009-01092-4 Paperback
ISSN 2632-816X (online)
ISSN 2632-8151 (print)

Additional resources for this publication at www.cambridge.org/turchi

Teaching with Interactive Shakespeare Editions

Elements in Shakespeare and Pedagogy

DOI: 10.1017/9781009024105

First published online: November 2023

Laura B. Turchi

Arizona State University

Author for correspondence: Laura B. Turchi, laura.turchi@gmail.com

ABSTRACT: This Element presents three case studies of interactive digital editions of Shakespeare incorporated into classroom teaching: *WordPlay Shakespeare*, *PerformancePlus*, and *myShakespeare*. Each interactive edition combines the text of a Shakespeare play with a recorded performance. The case studies seek to understand whether and how interactive Shakespeare editions support ambitious teaching, where students are expected to engage in authentic academic tasks, experience social learning (dialogic rather than didactic), and demonstrate their new knowledge through meaningful assessments. In our time of pandemic and considerable public contention over equity and justice, ambitious teaching further requires attention to the whole selves of students – their psychological and social development as well as their intellectual attainment. This Element examines the opportunities that interactive digital editions give teachers, software developers, and scholars to connect Shakespeare's works to twenty-first-century students.

KEYWORDS: Shakespeare pedagogy, multimodal digital texts, interactive editions, Shakespeare adaptations, ambitious teaching

ISBNs: 9781009010924 (PB), 9781009024105 (OC)

ISSNs: 2632-816X (online), 2632-8151 (print)

Contents

1 Digital Tools, Shakespeare, and Ambitious Teaching 1

2 Teaching with *WordPlay Shakespeare:* A Case
of Increased Reading Independence 23

3 Teaching with *PerformancePlus*: A Case of Theatrical
Productions Supporting Meaning-Making 43

4 Teaching with *myShakespeare*: A Case of Starting
Meaningful Conversations 62

5 Three Case Studies for Ambitious Teaching 84

References 97

Supplementary video files are available at
www.cambridge.org/turchi

1 Digital Tools, Shakespeare, and Ambitious Teaching

My father was a systems analyst, which helps explain why he was an early adopter of devices and gadgets that predated the home computer. He was forever tinkering with electronic components and imagining his workload automated while I was elsewhere, probably reading. Yet when I became a (US) high school teacher, I too embraced new technologies (and became locally infamous when three adolescents used my scanner – then a very cool new tool for the yearbook staff – to reproduce *Playboy* centrefolds). My enthusiasm for technology for teaching and learning led me to vote against mandating Shakespeare for every student in their senior year. Despite my love for British literature, I believed we needed more space in the curriculum for media classes, and something had to go. The department vote pitched visual literacies and student creativity against the seriousness and college preparation represented by Shakespeare. Shakespeare won.

To my mind, supporting new media meant offering unenthusiastic literature students a way to meet requirements using the tools and content that interested them; my colleagues saw a vote for Shakespeare as a vote for maintaining high expectations for secondary education. Neither side was wrong.

In a kind of Zen koan, the education of advanced learners (15–20 years old) is often perplexing: Do you teach the subject? Or teach the students? The work of promoting serious academic engagement without ignoring the learning interests, preferences, and needs of young adults has been called many things, including impossible. A more helpful framework that has emerged in formal research on classrooms is *ambitious teaching*. Learners are found to thrive in ambitious classrooms because there they experience authentic academic tasks, social learning, and meaningful assessments. Ambitious teaching strategies, as discussed in this Element, enable students to gain academic knowledge without sublimating their identities to unquestioned norms: instead, students are nurtured as critical thinkers. To teach Shakespeare ambitiously requires both an expansive knowledge of complex texts and a commitment to students puzzling out meanings for themselves through the means they are inclined to use. And so: interactive digital editions of Shakespeare.

This Element presents three case studies of interactive digital editions of Shakespeare incorporated into classroom teaching at the high school and university level. Each interactive edition combines the text of a Shakespeare play with a performance to be viewed or heard. The reader/viewer enjoys many navigational affordances, entering or accessing information without a prescribed sequence, just as one might utilize a critical print edition (choosing when to read supplementary essays, check footnotes, consult references). The central text is organized by acts and scenes, but additional notes, commentary, and most importantly performances offer digressions, elaborations, and alternative pathways through the play. The case studies in this Element include examples of the glosses, translations, synopses, character guides, notes, supplemental information, and study-guide-like questions (and answers) that students can access.

Each case study considers whether and how the interactive Shakespeare edition supports ambitious teaching. Support is evidenced in multiple ways. Does the edition take over some of the foundational work that a teacher often must provide when assigning a Shakespeare play? Not the close reading, but the initial reading: the necessary familiarity with characters and situations that sometimes teachers treat as an end in itself. It appears that with an interactive edition students can make meaning from a text on their own, choosing textual tools and consulting their peers, rather than depending passively on a teacher's explanations. Does the digital edition expand and complicate the reader/viewer's thinking about a Shakespeare play? The more typical approach may be to reduce and simplify a play, helping students to know 'the gist'. But to what purpose? The three case studies analyse the ways that the interactive editions promote critical thinking about the designs and decisions required for creating an edition of a text and presenting a performance. As detailed in Section 1.1, what's *ambitious* about ambitious teaching is that students are expected to engage in authentic academic tasks, experience social learning (dialogic rather than didactic), and demonstrate their new knowledge through meaningful assessments and assignments.

These case studies interrogate how interactive editions make Shakespeare accessible for learners who have a wide range of abilities. The case studies also note where the embedded Shakespeare production represents identities as diverse as the students, and thus helps make the play relevant to contemporary classrooms. In our time of pandemic and considerable public contention over equity and justice, ambitious teaching further requires attention to the whole selves of students – their psychological and social development as well as their intellectual attainment. This Element examines the opportunities that interactive digital editions give teachers, software developers, and scholars to connect Shakespeare's works to twenty-first-century students.

1.1 Research on Ambitious Teaching

1.1.1 Authentic Academic Tasks

Multidisciplinary educational research has worked to delineate the combination of teacher knowledge and teaching skills that underlies ambitious practices. These practices result in instructional designs (in classroom environments, teaching strategies, and curricular choices) that make student learning the priority: the central ambition is that *all* students learn. Students experience ambitious teaching when class activities and assignments offer multiple paths to gain academic knowledge, especially the terminology of a subject, and the tools of the discipline. Magdalene Lampert and colleagues explain that to do this, students need to acquire the basic skills of a discipline while they encounter more complicated ideas within it (2013, p. 226). Students develop knowledge about a subject through taking on authentic tasks: as Lampert and Filippo Graziani report, students doing so become more sophisticated in the academic language they use to communicate their ideas (2009, p. 492). In studying literature, for instance, students might learn to use literary terms such as metaphor or synecdoche to make sense of how Iago persuades Othello to his ruin.

1.1.2 Social Learning

Ambitious teaching taps into the power of social learning: students engage as group members in activities that take advantage of their heterogeneity. According to Lorrie Shepard, shared assignments draw on different kinds of talents, making room for collaborating across different ability levels (Shepard 2021, p. 29). Authentic teaching means managing authentic group work, accepting what Lampert and colleagues describe as social risks for teachers and for their students (2011, p. 228). The teacher must be willing to risk following student interests rather than a lockstep curriculum. Mark Windschitl and colleagues find that students are enabled to take risks and feel stretched by new ideas when they experience a relational space in a classroom for role playing, group work, and other social learning (2011, p. 1312).

The social learning analysed in this Element potentially happens in theatre-based classroom instruction, despite the digital nature of the editions. Teaching Shakespeare through dramatic pedagogies, teachers and theatre artists create physical and emotional space that allows embodied experimentation with a play text: these cases consider whether such enactments are still possible and useful when students use interactive editions. With theatre-based classroom activities students enact text for the discovery of wonderful ideas, as Lisa Schneier (2021) describes, through 'playfulness, fun, choice, action, and movement' (p. 72). Theatre-based classroom practices also offer opportunities for opening up classroom discussions on student identity as well as artistic expression,[1] as discussed in Section 2.1.

1.1.3 Assessments That Gauge Learning that Matters

Lorrie Shepard's work on assessment emphasizes that ambitious teaching values the learning of 'all kinds of students' (2021, p. 28). Rather than reducing content acquisition to right or wrong answers, authentic tasks and exercises capture complex learning. Ambitious teaching uses the results of such assessments formatively, as Jessica Thompson and colleagues explain, enabling the teacher to adjust and modify plans and activities to boost student progress (2013, p. 574). Consequently, teachers need substantial knowledge of, and the capacity to access resources for, alternative pathways for students to gain understanding: according to Deborah Loewernberg Ball and Francesca M. Forzani, ambitious teaching does not simply repeat or water down material for students to succeed on a test (2009, p. 500). The central goal of socially and intellectually ambitious teaching is student sense-making.

---

[1] See Ayanna Thompson and Laura Turchi, *Teaching Shakespeare with Purpose* chapter 4, 'Embodiement: What Is It (Not)?'

The success of a teaching unit built around a Shakespeare play would not be measured by student regurgitation of characters and plot points.

Instead, ambitiously teaching Shakespeare with an interactive digital edition should mean that students make sense of the play independently and with their peers. They access glosses, lexicons, and dictionaries to expand their understanding of the words, perhaps creating a shared edition that clarifies and represents what matters most to their interpretation. Students view performances and related artefacts that enable them to see the work as drama and have a window into the making of theatre. They work together to enact the text, deepening their familiarity with the language as they pronounce the words, imagining, and embodying the emotion and movement suggested. Through activities and facilitated discussions students could consider the cultural context of the play at its writing and through history, while finding and investigating resonances in their own lives. With ambitious teaching and an interactive digital edition, the sense students make of a Shakespeare work would be grounded in who they are, stretching them to imagine the other lives, other voices represented in the play, as well as those that are not (and students could be encouraged to think about *why*).

If this seems like a lot, it is. Isolated individuals taking on ambitious teaching requires what Magdalene Lampert and colleagues decry as a 'herculean and idiosyncratic' archetype of teachers (2013, p. 17). Jessica Thompson and colleagues note that student teachers are understandably dismayed at the prospect of ambitiously teaching on their own (2019, p. 3). In no way is 'ambitious' meant here to be an evaluative measure of teacher practices. Instead, this Element systematically considers whether and how interactive digital editions of Shakespeare plays can support the high academic expectations and deep student engagement characteristic of ambitious teaching.

1.2 Teaching the Whole Selves of Students

Gail Richmond and colleagues have raised concerns that ambitious teaching's focus on student acquisition of academic knowledge and the tools of a discipline may not 'sufficiently value the cultural backgrounds of learners' nor 'highlight culturally bound lived experiences' (2017, p. 432). They call for culturally sustaining pedagogies (citing Django Paris) to make ambitious teaching truly inclusive. Paris's point, in urging educators beyond culturally relevant or responsive practices, is to promote schooling that embraces linguistic, literate, and cultural pluralism (2012, p. 93). Student identities and homes, their communities, the whole selves that they bring to our classrooms, must be part of how and why they acquire academic knowledge and skills.

If a classroom means to nurture the whole selves of individual students, ambitious teaching can make no assumption – spoken or otherwise – that students all share experiences that lead them to trust authority, for instance. There needs to be room for students who experience food or housing insecurity to express dissatisfaction with characters whose privileged lives give them immunity from the consequences of impulsive choices. Students may want to raise religious objections to witches or demons, or too much make-believe. They may not share expectations about parental authority or the importance of obedience. They may bring experiences with mental illness or dementia that will be deeply relevant to their literary interpretations. Students may have strong opinions about biracial marriage or LGBTQ relationships. The lived experiences and perspectives of students are important to how they respond to literature and make sense of it.

Each of the interactive editions discussed here embeds productions in which students can see different races and ethnicities represented. The cases that follow identify where the editions directly support teachers in highlighting colour-blind, or perhaps colour-rich, casting decisions. The sections that follow further indicate places where such classroom dialogue could arise, and where editions do or could include prompts or starting places for such discussions. As Ayanna Thompson and I argue, the key is to interrogate students' preconceived ideas about what Shakespeare characters look and sound like (2016, p. 78). Such interrogations are a part of ambitious teaching.

Students have academic identities as well, and teachers may only know them through the limited perspective of their interest and ability with schoolwork. There are teachers who believe that Shakespeare is 'for everybody', and yet their ideas about Shakespeare teaching may need to be questioned. When teachers say that students love *Romeo and Juliet*, it is worth asking *which* students they mean – the honours students, the 'good readers'? One literacy coach interviewed about schools that had – and had not – adopted one of the interactive editions explained that some English departments in the district decided that Shakespeare plays were not worth the effort required to teach them, that there was too much resistance from students who 'only need to watch the movie'.

In my experiences of many US English language arts classrooms, teaching Shakespeare can mean a classroom of students who passively listen, following along the play text as recorded by actors. Reaching the end of a scene, a teacher will ask, 'Any questions?' or 'What just happened?' and get back little. Often the teacher then tells the class what they have heard, and they move on. Or students read scenes aloud, without preparation or guidance for pronunciation (just a teacher's frequent corrections), and most students (especially those who don't volunteer to read) literally do not know what is being said. Teachers who provide *NoFear Shakespeare* editions or other modern translations may claim that 'just getting students to read' is challenge enough. Students need teachers who are more ambitious for their learning. Increasing opportunities for more students to encounter and understand Shakespeare plays is social justice. This is not about what Shakespeare per se can do for students, but what students gain when they have confidence that they are capable of reading and thinking about complex ideas.

1.3 Why Combining Text and Performance Matters

The interactivity of the editions discussed in these cases may matter most because students have increased agency, have choices among the features or buttons that intrigue them, as they figure out what is going on in a play and why. The cases in this Element further examine the evidence for how interactive digital editions might help students recognize the *intentionality* of theatre arts through critical thinking about productions. Each of the interactive editions includes cast lists, production credits, and other features that might remind students of the collaborative work of theatre and film. The embedded productions should enable them to consider the endless series of choices and decisions by directors, designers, actors, crew, and more that culminate in a Shakespeare production. Paying attention to the making of art should also help a student untangle a particular production from the play's text. Many teachers have read student papers about Romeo and Juliet in a swimming pool and Tybalt shooting Mercutio, conflating Baz Luhrmann's *Romeo + Juliet* with 'the play'. Ambitious teaching can guide students to articulate their reactions to performances, analysing interpretations by comparing productions.

Mary Ellen Dakin's *Reading Shakespeare Film First* is a useful place for English teachers to find advice and ideas for teaching students to recognize camera angles and other cinematographic strategies that make filmmaking an art in its own right (2012, p. 28). She presents activities that help students see that reading a film requires learning a new language and unlocking 'a medium that deliberately effaces itself' (2012, p. 31). Students can learn to recognize the craft, the intentionality, of a multitude of performance choices. Each of the interactive editions addressed in this Element involves all those choices, from camera placement to sound capture, lighting and costumes, settings and more. Ambitious teaching encourages students to ask many questions of these choices: How is the eye being told what is most important to look at? When and how does a production show the characters, and how closely do we see them? What is the impact?

With ambitious teaching, students might consider too the work of designing and developing a software platform to become an interactive edition, one that allows navigation of the play text, performance, and all the supporting materials. Students can think about and perhaps try their hands at the substantial textual work of writing synopses, choosing what to gloss, and other responsibilities of an editor. Not every English class will talk about the 'behind the scenes' work, but it is good citizenship to acknowledge labour (and the computing and design work that might be interesting to some students). Ambitious teaching builds the academic habit of critical thinking: an interactive digital edition of Shakespeare represents almost endless points of decision making about the text and the performance.

1.4 Why 'Editions'?

Noam Lior's work suggests that the 'depth and breadth of scholarly undertaking, and in particular a level of bibliographic competence and discipline' are what define a Shakespeare edition (2019, p. 17). He acknowledges that there is no 'industry standard' for naming digital objects that combine text and performance. Lior is hesitant to call the embedded audio and video recordings *performances* at all, based on their not being live, but he offers a useful discussion of artists 'working at the intersection of theatre performance and digital technologies' and all the ways that mediation is decidedly not the same as live theatre (2019, p. 19). In Lior's analysis, which looks at two of the interactive editions discussed in this Element, some such editions may not be appropriate for more sophisticated readers because extensive scholarship is not part of their design. In the context of supporting ambitious teaching, however, 'edition' usefully refers to the software platform, including the text, the performance, and the auxiliary materials. Advanced edition learners who are new to taking Shakespeare seriously can hear the word *edition* as a reminder of the specialized work involved in preparing all these dimensions. Looking closely at the many decisions made in creating an interactive digital edition can enable advanced learners to consider the evolution of Shakespeare texts from the working scripts of Shakespeare the playwright to the authoritative editions today.

Anyone who writes about web pages, software platforms, and other digital interactive texts will recognize the challenge of describing all the links and non-linear progressions that are encompassed in these interactive Shakespeare editions. But the complexities of describing a Shakespeare text as printed and performed are already acknowledged by scholars. Jonathan Hope describes the 'three-dimensional networks of interdependent connections and recursive loops' of Shakespeare's grammar (2003, p. 3). Steven Orgel argues that the 1929 Cranach Press illustrated *Hamlet* edition with its representations of dramatic moments 'reconceives the book of the play as a performance and completes the play as a book' (2007, p. 310). Brett D. Hirsch and colleagues commiserate with performance critics who seek to use text to represent 'a rich and dynamic interplay of audio and visual stimuli, [and] a display of motion and emotion (ephemeral in the case of theatrical performance)' (2017, p. 1). Sonia Massai argues that a truly complete Shakespeare edition would need to be a 'Play(book)', potentially including the text of the play as performed and then printed, the revisions made to scripts and in reprints, and what she calls the 'textual network' that provides interpretive context (2017, p. 56). For this Element, an *interactive*

Video 1 The access page for the plays available in *WordPlay Shakespeare*.
Video file is available at www.cambridge.org/turchi

Video 2 The access page for the plays available in *PerformancePlus*. Video
file is available at www.cambridge.org/turchi

Video 3 The access page for the plays available in *myShakespeare*. Video file is available at www.cambridge.org/turchi

edition encompasses the set of strategies that an edition's creator has deployed to present a Shakespeare text and performance together with enough additional aids so that the reader can make it meaningful.

1.5 Other Digital Shakespeares Abound: *Why* These *Interactive Editions?*

This Element takes a systematic look at three interactive digital editions of Shakespeare: *WordPlay Shakespeare*, *PerformancePlus*, and *myShakespeare*. Laura Estill's Introduction to *Digital Resource Reviews* describes the plethora of Shakespeare and Shakespeare-adjacent online texts, noting their differences based on 'what different users value: interface, textual integrity, features, editorial apparatus, and so on' (2019, p. 167). The interactive digital editions reported in this Element were selected for their appropriateness for advanced learners and their potential for supporting ambitious teaching. They are the digital tools most useful for students who have not before been required to engage in close reading of a Shakespeare text and collaborative meaning-making (as ambitious teaching demands).

What seem not particularly appropriate for *teaching* advanced learners are the ubiquitous Shakespeare 'explainers' available on YouTube. These include student-made projects as well as video commentaries offered by self-identified 'Shakespeare Professors' under the aegis of programmes claiming to make Shakespeare 'easy' like Course Hero[2] or Cliffs Notes[3]. Other websites and video links offer synopses and modern language translations (including the online version of *NoFear Shakespeare*[4]). For better or worse, students do find these sites on their own and use them as they must. Emergent multilingual students and seriously struggling readers can indeed benefit from consulting straightforward renditions of Shakespeare's texts, and as we will see, such translations are included in two of the interactive digital editions detailed in this Element. But ambitious teaching means building student comfort with the idea that there is not a single or 'easy' answer to interesting questions that a class takes on collaboratively. Ideally students should become impatient with the matter-of-fact and would-be authoritative pronouncements of 'explainers' that offer so little nuance. They should reject (or at least want to argue about) overly simplistic explanations of character motivations, such as the Sparks Notes conclusion that in *The Merchant of Venice*, 'the fact that the most avaricious, greedy character ends up having lost both his physical wealth as well as his daughter and his religion warns against the dangers of excessive greed'.[5] Ambitious teaching requires better resources than these.

Some of the widely available online Shakespeare 'Explainers' include computer-generated animations as illustrations, some depicting characters without faces who making flailing 'acting' gestures reminiscent of Mark Twain's Duke and Dauphin. This is not to reject animations completely: there are clever animated segments in some of the titles in the *myShakespeare* interactive editions analysed in this Element. There is also

[2] www.coursehero.com   [3] www.cliffsnotes.com

[4] www.sparknotes.com/shakespeare/

[5] www.sparknotes.com/shakespeare/merchant/character/shylock/

Shakespeare in Bits [shakespeareinbits.com], which offers a series of Shakespeare plays that are animated and narrated in an interactive digital edition. Analysing the illustrated performance as a further adaptation of Shakespeare is beyond the scope of this Element. In addition, the stance of developers towards why Shakespeare needs to be accessible is problematic: 'the weight of opinion for generations is well summed up by Shakespeare's contemporary Ben Johnson [*sic*] who said that Shakespeare was "for all time." His themes and explorations of the human condition are universal. But without accessibility, their relevance may never be revealed to the student'[6]. To claim that making Shakespeare's words more understandable will make a play more relevant is to underestimate the work of ambitious teaching.

If some digital resources are too limited to engage the advanced learner, the archival sites such as OpenSource Shakespeare[7] or Internet Shakespeare Editions[8] are likely too much. The latter proclaims, 'Our aim is to inspire a love of Shakespeare's works by delivering open-access, peer-reviewed Shakespeare resources with the highest standards of scholarship, design, and usability.' Unfortunately, ambitious teaching at the secondary level is not well supported when a site requires teachers to preview and curate materials to make access appropriate for all students. Similarly, university students in introductory courses may be overwhelmed without more guided exploration. As this Element argues that close reading of a Shakespeare text is essential, archival searching offers interesting supplemental work. Advanced learners may become enthralled chasing the astonishing resources available online, but first, or at least simultaneously (in an ambitious teaching design), they need a solid experience with the Shakespeare text itself. It is important to remember that close reading is real work, and it may not feel as enticing as gorgeous costume collections or intriguing production designs or the history of particular daggers or the foibles of royalty or even how to get tickets to a production at Shakespeare's Globe. It would be a useful inquiry to determine how much students need to know first about what they are looking for, or how much rudimentary

---

[6] https://shakespeareinbits.com/educators/ [7] www.opensourceshakespeare.org/
[8] https://internetshakespeare.uvic.ca

knowledge of the text is required for productive searching. The text-annotating initiatives described below offer some insights.

Clearly, excellent digital editions and collections of Shakespeare materials can be useful secondary sources to the curious advanced learner who wants to expand their understanding through artefacts or facsimiles. When students have a reasonable knowledge of a Shakespeare text and a growing understanding of performative choices, they may want to explore the MIT Global Shakespeares Video and Performance Archive[9] or Drama Online[10]. Even if advanced learners are only ready to dabble in performance or reception studies, it is valuable for them to see worldwide perspectives on a play and its resonances in other cultures. Comparative exercises, where students look carefully at relationships between text and differing performances, build critical perspectives. Teachers as well as advanced learners may further discover the performances available through National Theatre Live and other online venues (especially as these have expanded as a result of the pandemic). The accompanying online 'Teaching Packs' that the National Theatre, Shakespeare's Globe, the Royal Shakespeare Company, and other theatre companies offer can support ambitious teaching with on-your-feet activities and interesting tie-ins to specific productions. *PerformancePlus*, the interactive digital edition from the Stratford Festival described in this Element, includes similar materials and supporting videos.

In US high schools it is not unusual for graduating seniors to be expected to complete a major paper as evidence of their knowledge of research processes (source searching, note taking, citational practices, organizational strategies, and more). Given their crammed schedules, students taking multiple advanced placement courses may 'double dip' this requirement and practise their research skills on literary theory. The result can be a disturbingly random cherry-picking of scholarship in support of a thesis, where students have little idea that they are looking at academic scholarly dialogue that literally spans centuries. Thus online Shakespeare sites that focus on collecting and curating research, or creating digital editions of specific works, are not well suited to the advanced learners described here. The works of scholarship that students encounter on these

[9] https://globalshakespeares.mit.edu [10] www.dramaonlinelibrary.com

sites are very much complex texts themselves, and most advanced learners will require guidance to make sense of them.

Advanced learners could become interested in some of the scholarly quasi–social media networks that are encouraged around online Shakespeare editions. For instance, *PlayShakespeare.com* has an interface that identifies 'friends' and offers 'badges' in an effort to promote online discussion. It would certainly be a wonderful outcome of ambitious teaching if an advanced learner became interested – and confident – enough in a specific domain of Shakespeare scholarship to join in. James Paul Gee describes online communities of like-minded people as 'affinity groups' (2017, p. 27) and advanced learners can definitely expand their sense of the world of scholarship if they find a place in one. No matter how ambitious the teaching, however, it seems unlikely that every student would be interested in joining this kind of scholarly community around a Shakespeare text.

Offering access to a different kind of scholarly community, Rachael Deagman Simonetta led the creation of *CoLab*, a peer-to-peer digital learning environment for Shakespeare studies at the University of Colorado (2022, p. 25). *CoLab* gives students practise in text editing and using research databases as they dig deep in the meanings and etymologies of specific words in Shakespeare's plays, and they share their discoveries online in annotations using text-encoding software. Students advance from *Oxford English Dictionary* explorations to looking at facsimiles and understanding orthological practices together, to creating transcriptions, all important entry points to the work of digital humanities. The interactive editions being scrutinized in this Element have parallel annotations to the kinds students create in the *CoLab*, and seeing this work is a potential window for advanced learners to think about how editions are made, and the levels of scholarship required.

There are digital editions and Shakespeare collections behind paywalls associated with university publishers and textbook firms. These may have, or could be developing, comparable features to those discussed here, and thus could be supportive of ambitious teaching. More typically, however, textbooks focus on illustrating Shakespeare texts – for instance, offering interesting pictures from productions and even pointing the reader to notice performative decisions that are captured in the still photo. Many online textbooks do offer auditory features, so that students can hear a Shakespeare play read, if not enacted, as they read along. *WordPlay Shakespeare* requires purchasing or licensing for school use, and some of its materials for *Romeo and Juliet* have been incorporated in the College Board's Pre-AP curriculum. As noted below, the edition's creator, Alexander Parker of the New Book Press, has given free access to interested teachers across the United States, even before the Covid pandemic.

The three interactive digital editions being scrutinized in this Element necessarily represent just a dip into the river of technological innovation for teaching and learning. Laura Estill described digital Shakespeare texts that are 'constantly maintained and updated or fall into oblivion' (2019, p 169). The analysis presented in this Element owes a debt to Noam Lior's dissertation analysis of the affordances of seven digital Shakespeare editions, including two of the ones analysed here. Lior's scholarship offers invaluable perspectives as dramaturg and producer of an ambitious interactive digital edition titled *Shakespeare at Play*, which unfortunately is no longer available. Similarly *Heuristic Shakespeare*, launched by Heuristic Media in 2012 with an edition of *The Tempest* starring Sir Ian Mckellen, has not yet delivered on its promise of a series of thirty-seven Shakespeare plays. Another interactive edition was *Luminary*, a collaboration between the Folger Shakespeare Library and Simon & Schuster publishing, an app that was discontinued because of distribution challenges. Table 1 lists the Shakespeare plays available in each of the digital editions analysed in this Element.

1.6 Methodologies for the Cases

I first learned of interactive digital editions of Shakespeare when a local district agreed to have English language arts teachers voluntarily explore using *WordPlay Shakespeare*. I met with Alexander Parker and a secondary English support specialist to talk about what they were learning. Parker told of his repeated experience when demonstrating a *WordPlay Shakespeare* edition: teachers wanted to know 'what to do with it'. While this reaction no longer surprised him, it did lead him to wonder about teachers' ideas and purposes in teaching Shakespeare and what role *WordPlay* should take in their classrooms. We schemed together about answering these questions. I gained permission from the district to carry out interviews and focus groups with teachers who had adopted *WordPlay Romeo and Juliet* and *Macbeth*; with the

Table 1 Three digital editions and the Shakespeare play each offers

WordPlay Shakespeare	*PerformancePlus*	*myShakespeare*
Romeo and Juliet	*Romeo and Juliet*	*Romeo and Juliet*
Macbeth	*Macbeth*	*Macbeth*
A Midsummer Night's Dream	*A Midsummer Night's Dream*	*A Midsummer Night's Dream*
	Hamlet	*Hamlet*
	Othello	
	Tempest	
	King Lear	
		Julius Caesar
		The Taming of the Shrew

help of the secondary specialist, I was able to hear about teaching strategies in classrooms of students with wide-ranging levels of literacy abilities. I also traded my time, and shared resources for teaching *Midsummer Night's Dream* in return for later classroom observations of eighth-grade students using the edition, including an amazing day of films/creative projects supported, and sometimes inspired, by *WordPlay*.[11] These experiences in classrooms informed my interviews with current users for this Element as well as my analysis of the affordances of the editions for ambitious teaching.

Each of the creative teams that developed the interactive editions discussed in this Element has nurtured strong partnerships with teachers: The Stratford Festival has a formal Teacher (and Student) Advisory Council, and both *myShakespeare* and *WordPlay Shakespeare* were, pre-Covid,

---

[11] That case study is available: Laura B. Turchi (2020). Shakespeare e-Books engage students and support ambitious teaching. *Research in Drama Education* Themed Issue: Teaching Shakespeare: Digital Processes. https://doi.org/10.1080/13569783.2019.1687290

regular exhibitors and participants at US English teacher conferences and meetings of literature associations. Each of the developers of the interactive editions in this Element offers different aids to teachers to make the most of the tools, although their relatively small-scale professional development offerings[12] are not required for using the digital platforms.

Working with the creators of the three interactive editions, and through my own network from previous studies and initiatives, I identified teachers who used a given digital edition and were willing to speak about their experiences. Approximately hour-long interviews, mostly of individual teachers, took place over the winter holidays of 2020–21, using and recording on Zoom. This was the end of a semester where online or hybrid teaching was the new normal in North America. After the previous spring's emergency change-over to virtual classrooms, teachers had found some equilibrium in routines and increasingly familiar digital tools. Nonetheless, most observational education research was at a standstill. Ambitious teaching of Shakespeare plays in an entirely online context has not been studied.

Mary M. Kennedy and colleagues detail the many variables that influence what a teacher does in specific moments of teaching, and how rarely these teacher choices or 'moves' can be mapped back to a particular training or initiative in instruction or curriculum (2019, p. 140). In writing this Element, I asked teachers how the interactive editions fit into their usual practices. In order to understand the whirlwind of activity – all the decisions, calculations, and choices – that a Shakespeare unit of study represents, I listened to teachers as they made the time to recollect incidents, articulate opinions, and offer rationales. Thus each case is able to describe the interactive digital edition in use and the possibilities for ambitious teaching that result.

The contextual realities of the Covid pandemic are worth remembering. Before, literature classrooms could use learning management systems to organize student reading and writing assignments, support student collaboration through shared drafts and annotations, and facilitate student-to-student review and commentary. Many schools housed equipment and software for

---

[12] The Stratford Festival, which created *PerformancePlus*, offers extensive professional development for teaching Shakespeare, but the focus is not the use of the digital edition: see Section 3.

collaborative multimedia projects. But with the move to virtual teaching, online platforms became the medium for instruction, with 'classroom' time redefined as synchronous Zoom or Microsoft Teams or Google Meets sessions. The classrooms of the teachers I interviewed were largely online; some instruction was synchronous, some not. Some teachers could only communicate with students by way of assignments given and collected through a learning management system, and this they reported was a poor substitute for giving directions, clarifying expectations, and facilitating discussion. Group work, especially creative projects, was necessarily restricted because many students were house-bound. The inequities of online access are well documented. Any interesting novelty from an unfamiliar online platform – like an interactive edition of Shakespeare – became less enticing. Indeed, some interviewees had all but given up on teaching Shakespeare, feeling that the amount of teaching the text required was beyond what they could muster under the circumstances. Other teachers, a few who had already taught with an interactive digital edition pre-pandemic, found them extremely valuable. This Element seeks to explain how and why.

At times I use the descriptors of 'most' or 'some' teachers loosely to indicate multiple mentions or echoes of ideas about different features in the digital editions, or different ways to use them. The joke goes that the plural of anecdote is data, and this Element represents some social science methodology without claiming the rigour of control groups or other quasi-experimental endeavours. As I discuss in the final section, the real-time classroom use of digital editions for teaching Shakespeare deserves much more study.

Rather than defining or explaining 'ambitious teaching' to the interview subjects, the interview questions queried the teachers on their use of the interactive editions of Shakespeare in their classrooms. The open-ended prompts included:

1. How did you integrate [digital edition] into your teaching (if as a part of a larger Shakespeare play unit, for example – how did it fit into your teaching approach?)
2. Describe the ways you talked about/discussed (with the students) the text and/or the performance offered by [digital edition]
3. Were your students required to use [the interactive edition]? Why or why not?

4. Did you see or hear student reactions as they were introduced to or used the interactive edition?
5. Could you tell, informally or possibly on subsequent assignments or assessments, what impact the interactive edition had on student understanding of the play?
6. What advice would you give other teachers about using the interactive edition, and/or what plans you have for future use of it?

For data analysis, I categorized responses by the tools that teachers mentioned within the interactive editions, and how they described their students' using, for instance, the glosses and definitions, synopses, and the modern language translations. I collected and compared ways that the teachers talked about assigning the editions as part of their classroom instruction, what they witnessed in terms of engagement, and the markers they used for student success. I sent drafts to these teachers, asking for their feedback and permission to name them. Everyone agreed to be listed. The names of the teachers I interviewed are identified in each section. Because my sample size was small, I chose not to cite individual quotations, but instead described opinions anonymously to portray teacher perspectives and maintain confidentiality.

1.7 Framework for Analysis: Evidence Ambitious Teaching Is Supported by Interactive Digital Editions

To understand the ambitious use of interactive digital editions of Shakespeare, I applied a framework of research-established characteristics of ambitious teaching to the descriptions teachers provided of their classroom deployment of each edition, as delineated below.

Authentic Academic Tasks

- Evidence/examples that interactive digital editions focus students on academic texts and academic language.
- Descriptions of how and why interactive editions supported students making sense of the original Shakespeare text, including their use of synopses, translations of texts, and glosses for unfamiliar words or unexpected usages.

- Descriptions of how the integration of performance with the text in the edition impacted their instructional decisions and the learning that seemed to result.
- Comparisons of the embedded performance to other film or theatre performances used in the unit (or in previous Shakespeare units).
- Perceived opportunities for opening the art of drama/theatre-making to students.

Social Learning

- Descriptions of theatre-based classroom practices used in tandem with the interactive digital edition.

Assessments of Genuine Learning

- Observed and described ways that students develop academic language (including through writing assignments) in using the interactive editions.

The Whole Selves of Students

- Described beliefs about how the interactive digital editions helped more, or different, or unexpected students to understand a Shakespeare play.
- The extent to which the digital editions provide useful cultural contexts for the Shakespeare play.

1.8 Limitations to the Research

Even in focusing closely on only three interactive digital editions, this Element cannot account for every digital tool within each edition, as some are added or deleted without leaving much of a trace. As this goes to press, each edition is being revamped or augmented.

The geographical frame of reference for this Element is Shakespeare teaching in North America, including teachers in Canada and Mexico. I also benefitted from consultations with teachers in England who talked about Shakespeare instruction and digital tools there, even though I was unable to find anyone using the editions in this Element. The developers of the editions are based in the United States and Canada, and each has metrics indicating worldwide logons and adoptions.

My access to teachers did not include watching them teach, nor reviewing the work of their students.[13] In Section 5, opinions I can cite from my own students were captured in informal surveys, exit tickets (brief reflections on learning at the end of a lesson), and feedback after trying out some of the interactive editions.

Despite the ubiquitous appearance of Shakespeare plays in textbooks and on curriculum lists, few, if any, of the teachers in this Element are accountable for what their students can specifically 'do' with a Shakespeare play. Unlike some levels of secondary education in England and Australia, there is no expectation at the national or state or even district level that students will complete a formal assessment that showcases their ability to recall or independently work with a Shakespeare text.[14] Sometimes teaching Shakespeare is something that a US teacher does in spite of, rather than because of, standardized testing expectations. Some teachers wager that the work students do to understand a Shakespeare play transfers in some way to their achievement on standardized tests; others limit teaching Shakespeare plays to only those perceived as academically able.

While this Element means to celebrate the artistry and practical science in teaching challenging literature, it cannot provide a comprehensive plan for incorporating digital editions in a classroom. The teachers were not asked to catalogue every aspect of their instructional approach to teaching a Shakespeare play, or to describe the entire curriculum landscape students navigated with supplemental materials and complementary texts. Instead, our conversations focused on how teachers incorporated the interactive editions into their

---

[13] I thank Julie Black, Natalia Bondar, and Thomas Keene Jr., teachers who shared their analyses of their students' work; and also Natalie Gibson, Elizabeth Partridge, and anonymous others from my English and Education courses, who agreed to have their work excerpted.

[14] Not even the College Board's Advanced Placement examinations, which may earn students college credit, *require* Shakespeare. 'Our obligation, our joy as teachers of AP English is to accompany our students on a journey across cultures and centuries, introducing them along the way to the most interesting texts and characters we can find.' https://apcentral.collegeboard.org/courses/ap-english-literature-and-composition/classroom-resources/art-teaching-ap-english-literature

classroom practices, and how they saw their students use and respond to the tools. The sections that follow include references to teaching Shakespeare before, as well as during, the pandemic, and hopes and intentions for future uses of the interactive editions. This Element offers perspectives and suggests opportunities that a teacher – or a software developer, or a scholar – can consider when imagining ways Shakespeare plays can be taught ambitiously with twenty-first-century students.

2 Teaching with *WordPlay Shakespeare*: A Case of Increased Reading Independence

WordPlay Shakespeare, created as an e-book by The New Book Press, is an interactive edition designed to enhance reading a Shakespeare play.[15] *WordPlay* provides a performance directly next to and synchronized with the text. 'WordPlay: Now, Half the Page is a Stage' is its trademarked slogan. On most pages of *WordPlay*, the reader encounters the text on the left side of the screen, while a borderless window on the right side shows the performance, turning readers into viewers and listeners too. Jessica Bauman, the filmed production's director, described the early decision to create a performance that 'comfortably sits with the text', by offering a minimum of interpretive overlays. The foreword of each edition describes an 'elegant, minimalist aesthetic we hope underscores our unswerving dedication to the power and value of Shakespeare's text'.[16] Throughout the edition the platform emphasizes the 'bookness' of the reader's experience as the performance and script/text scroll together, stopping at the end of each page. There are three *WordPlay Shakespeare* plays: *Macbeth*, *A Midsummer Night's Dream*, and *Romeo and Juliet*.

As CEO of The New Book Press and creator of *WordPlay*, Alexander Parker's commitment to supporting its use in schools has been evident. Hundreds of US teachers have discovered *WordPlay Shakespeare* through the New Book Press vendor booth at the annual convention of the National

---

[15] There are three plays in the edition: *Macbeth*, *A Midsummer Night's Dream*, and *Romeo and Juliet*.

[16] Link to the New Book Press website http://jessicabauman.net/film/wordplay-shakespeare/

Council of Teachers of English (NCTE). Even those lured there first by free chocolate find thoughtful and informative conversation about new ways Shakespeare plays can make sense to students through watching the performance and reading the text at (approximately) the same time. In addition to sponsoring a booth at NCTE and other state-level conferences of English teachers, Parker has presented to associations of secondary curriculum specialists and others who guide textbook and resource adoptions for at least the last five years.

Teachers often express a personal connection to *WordPlay* because of Parker's help with troubleshooting technological issues as well as answering their questions about the different functions available. Parker regularly queries teachers and adds features based on their suggestions (as described in what follows). He has made commitments to individual schools and teachers, providing professional development sessions and listening to teachers describe those features most useful to their classrooms and their students. Parker has been willing to meet with their students, showing production pictures from the creation of *WordPlay*, and sharing 'behind-the-scenes' details. He met with my student teachers virtually, talking about his design intentions for *WordPlay* and providing free licenses for all. And during the pandemic Parker has generously given away licenses to schools and teachers, in part facilitated by Georgia Public Broadcasting. The early months of Covid saw a quadrupling of *WordPlay Shakespeare* use.

As I spoke to teachers from across the United States[17] in the winter of 2020, most were enjoying a holiday respite from the complications of online and hybrid teaching. Some had adopted *WordPlay* before the onset of the pandemic; others had recently used the free access from the Covid-response programme from the New Book Press. Teachers I spoke referred to *WordPlay Shakespeare* as a 'gift' and a 'lifesaver'.

Through the teacher commentary and analysis of the *WordPlay Shakespeare* editions that follow, there is evidence of potential support for ambitious teaching. *WordPlay* offers students authentic academic engagement, increasing access to understanding the plays and a synched production

---

[17] Many thanks to: Leonard Aguilar, Kathy Appleton, Jiji Baylis, Josh Cooper, Catherine Flores, Julie Goodloe, Benjamin Humeniuk, and Thomas Keene Jr.

where students can see themselves represented. Most notable in this case, teachers found that *WordPlay Shakespeare's* book-like interface increased independent student comprehension of the play text.

2.1 Authentic Academic Tasks

Students experience ambitious teaching when class activities and assignments offer multiple ways to gain academic knowledge, especially the terminology of a subject, and the tools of the discipline. While the defining design feature of the *WordPlay Shakespeare* platform (see Figure 1) is the paired performance and text on each e-page, there are embedded resources for finding out the meaning of words, for understanding the allusions and other references intended, and for reflecting on the relationship between the text and the performance.

Teachers witnessed directly or heard from students about a range of ways to use the edition to make meaning out of a Shakespeare play. Some teachers described giving students explicit directions for how to move through the play in ways that they believed made the most of the *WordPlay* platform. Some teachers reminded students about watching, reading, and looking at the summaries and glosses, etc., without specifying a particular sequence. Other teachers were more prescriptive, although they acknowledged they had no way of enforcing a particular approach. For instance, students might be urged to read along first, concentrating on the left side of the screen, and then go back to watch the characters in action. Other teachers recommended that students read the scene synopsis first; or wait to read the modern translation only when answering specific questions. It is interesting to imagine a research design that would track eye or mouse movements to gauge student interaction with the platform and perhaps tie it to student understanding. At the bottom of the performance side of each screen is a relatively easy-to-miss button[18] labelled 'More'. In interviews teachers sometimes described features that did not seem to be available to others. Over time I realized that the 'missing' features were ones

[18] Access to these additional screens feels somewhat hidden: at least one teacher I met had never seen those additional links, and as a result students were using *WordPlay* with a print edition of *NoFear Shakespeare* alongside, rather than accessing the available modern translation.

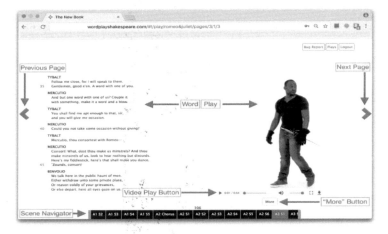

Figure 1 A diagram of *WordPlay* navigation

that the teachers had not yet seen for themselves. Of course there's a chance that their students have made these discoveries on their own.

2.1.1 Synopses and Character Identifications

WordPlay Shakespeare editions stop at the beginning of each act and scene for a synopsis (see Figure 2).

The synopsis organizes and previews what the reader is about to read/view, without imposing any interpretation. Thumbnail photographs highlight which character is which and who will be appearing in the scene. Numbers identify key moments in the scene, as illustrated here from *A Midsummer's Night Dream* Act 3 Scene 1:

> Puck stumbles into the Athenian townsmen (1) as they rehearse the play they intend to perform in front of the Duke, and mischievously transforms Bottom's head into that of a donkey (2). When the other actors see newly transformed Bottom (3), they flee. Awakened by the noise that Bottom makes as he stumbles around singing (to give

Act 3 Scene 4

SYNOPSIS

In the hopes of relieving the general misery, and as he explains to **Paris** (1) how things have gone so badly wrong – and also wholly unaware that **Juliet** is now married to **Romeo**, **Capulet** hits on the idea (2) that the wedding of **Paris** to **Juliet** should go ahead. After some calculations (3) he lands on a wedding in three day's time. He tells **Lady Capulet** to deliver the news to **Juliet** (4).

Figure 2 An example of a scene synopsis page

himself courage), Titania immediately falls in love with Bottom (4), and orders her fairies to look after him and bring him to her bower in the forest.

Beyond the synopses, *WordPlay* offers further interpretive possibilities in its additional embedded guides. The 'page summary' tab leads to a short text written in a conversational tone. These brief summaries invite the reader to make sense of the action and to see how specific Shakespeare lines make sense in their context. As *Midsummer* 3.1 starts, the summary reads:

In another part of the Athenian woods Peter Quince and his actors have gathered to rehearse their play, 'the most lamentable comedy of Pyramus and Thisbe'. Peter Quince feels that they have found a perfect spot to rehearse – a grassy area for the stage, and a hawthorn bush where actors can dress and also exit and enter from (This green plot shall be our stage, this hawthorn brake our tiring-house). Before they begin, Nick Bottom has – as usual – some important questions. He is worried first that

because Pyramus will pull out a sword to kill himself, the ladies
in the audience will be upset (Pyramus must draw a sword
to / kill himself; which the ladies cannot abide).

These commentaries take the reader beyond a simple who, what, and where
things are happening in the play but remain tightly connected to the words
of the play. The reader gains a general sense of what complex lines will
mean through seeing them embedded in that explanation.

2.1.2 Translations

WordPlay is unique among these interactive digital editions of Shakespeare
by offering translations to Spanish and Mandarin. These translations are
based on the modern English language versions, not the original
Shakespeare text. Multiple teachers told me that the Spanish text embedded
in *WordPlay* was 'a big help' for their bilingual students and described how
their students moved back and forth between the performance (in English)
and the Spanish notes. For all English versions of the play text, right
clicking on any word provides a direct dictionary look-up. While those
definitions take students out of the platform and thus the context of the play,
they do provide further handholds for student meaning-making.

Clicking on the 'More' button opens a modern English version of the
page. In some schools there is a mythology that reading Shakespeare 'evens
the playing field' for all students because the vocabulary and syntax are
equally difficult for everyone, including non-native English speakers.
Shakespearean syntax certainly challenges many students: one teacher
said her students liked watching *WordPlay* because despite 'how weird
they speak', the class could still understand what was going on. Usually
comprehension takes further teaching: 'We always thank Yoda', as one
teacher told me, for providing recognizable patterns.[19]

As a result of teacher requests, *WordPlay Romeo and Juliet* has added an
additional 'Modern +' translation that follows the original text with even

---

[19] See for instance www.grammardog.com/how-yoda-helps-students-master-
shakespeare and www.prestwickhouse.com/blog/post/2019/12/how-yoda-
helps-students-master-shakespeare.

simpler vocabulary and sometimes simplified syntax. Table 2 compares the three versions that a reader can choose among for Juliet's 'Gallop Apace' monologue, as an example.

While the actor portraying Juliet in this scene certainly communicates Juliet's impassioned impatience, the *WordPlay* editions offers significant commentary on it, as discussed further below.

2.1.3 Glosses and Notes on the Text

As both of the translations still preserve much of the diction and syntax, students may also need to access the gloss[es] provided under that tab. On the 'Gallop Apace' pop-up page they will learn:

1. apace – fast; quickly
2. steed – horse
4. And bring in cloudy night immediately. – make night-time come quickly
5. That th' runaway's – the out-of-control horses that draw the sun across the sky (thus bringing darkness sooner)

WordPlay interactive editions provide other kinds of clues to making sense of the text: identifying and explaining a malapropism, for instance *for there is not a more fearful wild-fowl than your lion living* in Act 3 Scene 1 *Midsummer*), and by noting words that were first coined by Shakespeare (with a reference to an authoritative supporting text). In *WordPlay Macbeth* there are 'Text Notes' that discuss Duncan's speech and the possible effects of his complex sentence structures on the audience's understanding of his character (Act 1 Scene 6).

Text notes in *Wordplay Macbeth* also reference specific literary devices or allusions, and sometimes explain idiomatic expressions. The reader's attention is pointed to repeating images, including this 'Bird Watch,' referencing birds throughout the play:

Macbeth (Act 1 Scene 2) Bird Watch

Notice the mention of two birds in the sergeant's description – the sparrow and the eagle. Although they form part of the sergeant's sarcastic point that Macbeth and Banquo were not remotely frightened

Table 2

WP Act 3 Scene 2	*WordPlay* Modern English	*WordPlay* Modern +
JULIET	JULIET	JULIET
Gallop apace, you fiery-footed steeds,	Gallop fast, you fiery-footed horses that pull the sun,	Gallop on, you fiery-footed horses that pull the sun,
Towards Phoebus' lodging; such a waggoner	Towards its home in the West; such a driver as	Towards its home in the West; A driver like
As Phaeton would whip you to the west,	The sun God's son Phaëton would whip you faster to the west,	The sun God's son Phaëton would whip you even faster to the west,
And bring in cloudy night immediately.	And bring cloudy night immediately.	And bring cloudy night immediately.
Spread thy close curtain, love-performing night,	Draw love-performing night like an enveloping curtain,	Bring in right now love-performing night, like an enveloping curtain,
That th' runaway's eyes may wink, and Romeo	So that th' runaway's eyes may wink, and Romeo	So that those runaway horses can pretend not to see what we do, and so that Romeo
Leap to these arms untalk'd of and unseen!	Can then leap into my arms unmentioned and unseen!	Can then leap into my arms unmentioned and unseen!

by the Norwegians, the birds form part of a broader motif throughout the play. There will be no fewer than thirteen birds mentioned in
the play.

To return to 'Gallop Apace' (*Romeo and Juliet* Act 3 Scene 2), *WordPlay*
offers additional guides to making sense of Juliet's speech, describing the
metaphorical language as 'Yet another series of images that suggest tragedy
ahead – here Juliet imagines Romeo getting cut into pieces when she dies,
and him becoming stars'. Students can find the words 'little stars' in the
speech, but not necessarily why Juliet's vision is 'grim', an interpretation
that might require further teacher prompting. The *WordPlay* notes provide
the (unnamed) editor's further analysis: 'There is also something unnerving
in the series of references to darkness in her soliloquy. Although she asks for
darkness to hide her activities with Romeo from people's eyes, there is also
the sense of darkness descending completely over her and Romeo.'
Wordplay explains why the reader could find these references *unnerving*:
'Even when Juliet raises the image of daylight with the image of Phaeton
racing across the sky with his father's sun chariot, we are mindful that
Phaeton's story ends in disaster' (and links to Wikipedia's *Phaeton* entry).'

To support critical thinking, students could be urged to notice that the
'we' of the edition is not identified: do they feel included in it? Students
might consider whether the embedded production communicates
both Juliet's impatience and something that is 'grim' or 'unnerving'.
A teacher could also ask students to look to whether the actor in
WordPlay performs the speech in a way that seems responsive to these
notes and this perspective, tying the text and performance together
further, as discussed below.

2.1.4 Text and Performance Combined

WordPlay Shakespeare editions are so committed to having the text paired
with the performance that opening any of the supplemental screens (discussed below) overlays and covers the performance screen. The performance stops – is literally obscured – as the reader consults the pop-up
screens for information. Students cannot, for instance, watch the performance
while reading the modern translation.

In *WordPlay*, professional actors perform on a white screen comparable to a black box theatre stage: there is no scenery and few props. The camera angle is usually fixed: characters are sometimes in a scene but out of sight, coming back into view only as they speak. Costuming is subtle: characters are largely in modern dress with accessories that help further distinguish them (plaid sashes in *Macbeth*, colour-coded family affiliations in *Romeo and Juliet*). On its website, *WordPlay Shakespeare* explains that reading the plays is necessarily difficult, and that understanding them requires the information 'contained in body language, oratory, emphasis, and positioning'. One teacher recounted how students referred to a character wearing red by saying, 'that's a Macbeth colour', clearly picking up on which character was aligning (or pretending to align) with whom and how the production was signalling alliances.

Wordplay includes prompts that point students to the production, reminding the reader about the relationship between what the text says and how it is being enacted. The reader/viewer is not told what to think but is invited to pay attention. For example, there is a commentary on 'Stagecraft' regarding the first appearance of the Mechanicals in *Midsummer*:

> Notice how the director has the actors go through their problem solving, and how they pause, think through and work through the problems. As a counterpoint, imagine simply reading this text. There are no instructions, *per se*, to pause, or move around as the actors do.

Of course, the Mechanicals are rehearsing a play to be performed within the play, and students will need to puzzle out who (or which character) is the director or is playing the director (see Figure 3). At the beginning of *Macbeth* 'Notes' offers a useful perspective on how the battle is not being staged, and yet is being experienced through its retelling by the Sergeant:

> *Macbeth* Act 1 Scene 2
> Note how the audience/reader is put in the picture (called the *mise en scene*) by dialogue in the play. This may be the

Figure 3 The Mechanicals in rehearsal in *WordPlay Shakespeare*

reason the wounded soldier speaks in so much detail – it gives us a great deal of information, even though it makes acting the part convincingly very hard.

WordPlay Shakespeare can help students draw comparisons between the embedded production and other filmed Shakespeare. The 'Notes' to *Romeo and Juliet* (Act 1 Scene 3) include leading the student to performance analysis, such as urging the reader to note the body language and other gestures by Juliet, her mother, and Nurse. Students are further prompted to compare *WordPlay*'s version with the Zeffirelli production (links provided), and *WordPlay* points to the music, camera work, costuming and more that 'convey the message of status and relative power amongst the three characters' that students might explore.

One teacher said *WordPlay* 'tees the students up' to see different film clips because they stop thinking that the text and performance are 'basically the same'. The 'Links' tab under 'More' provides the reader with access to alternative recordings of performances of the specific scene. *WordPlay Macbeth* provides links to a 1978 production directed by Philip Casson, starring Ian McKellen and Judi Dench. *WordPlay Romeo and Juliet* links to Franco Zeffirelli's Romeo and Juliet (1968) as well as a staged production filmed for Thames Television, UK (1976). *A Midsummer Night's Dream* does not include links to other productions. Some of the notes in *Romeo and Juliet* suggest comparisons between the *WordPlay* production and these clips, but for the most part the edition provides links without comment. Because some teachers have reported that YouTube (the host for these clips) is blocked in their schools, they do not assign students to watch these. Another teacher noted that students had no problems when they logged on from home during the pandemic.

Some teachers told me that they included clips from Zeffirelli and Luhrmann and modern adaptations like Junger's *Ten Things I Hate About You* in their Shakespeare teaching. They did not similarly describe leading students to think critically about the production embedded in *WordPlay*, except occasionally in response to a student comment or criticism of a particular actor. None mentioned drawing out comparisons between a movie and a recorded performance of a play.

2.1.5 Critical Thinking about How Art Is Made

There is a guide offered on the New Book Press website entitled 'Reading a Character Through Their Performance'[20] which encourages teachers to ask students about how they are judging a character based on a performance, on reading 'what "sort of person" a character is' based on physical actions as well as words. But this material is not embedded in any of the editions and, perhaps more importantly, no actors are named, and no reference is made to any broader directorial intentions that students might see enacted.

One teacher said that it was *WordPlay*'s interactivity, the reader's ability to navigate to individual moments within even a scene, that helped students start to see the intentionality of performances. Another teacher wanted

---

[20] www.thenewbookpress.com/resources/02-Romeo-and-Juliet—Characters-in-Performance.pdf

students to recognize that 'everything that an actor (or director) does is intentional/purposeful', that acting is not just 'natural' – and that actors are trying to communicate. *WordPlay Shakespeare* could do more to support such a critical perspective. The cast and crew are listed on credits pages at the opening of each *WordPlay*, but otherwise there is little done to remind the reader/viewer that the performance is being created for them by actors, or that their understanding is being mediated through the camera.

Teachers liked the functionality of the *WordPlay* platform because of how it allowed them to 'chunk it up', or look closely at particular sections, having students revisit key passages, of text and performance together. Some teachers described helping students think about the performance through reviewing a scene and asking them, 'would you do it that way?' For instance, when students wondered why Lady Macbeth 'jumped on' Macbeth on his arrival after battle, they wanted to know, 'is she just insane, or is there motivation?'

Teachers reported that *WordPlay Shakespeare* enabled them to choose specific scenes and instruct students to look for specific character moves that revealed more about what seemed to them to be happening: were the characters telling the truth? Were they serious in their expressed sorrow? Why were they becoming angry? One teacher said the subsequent class conversations were richer in specific examples from the text because the students were seeing, as well as reading, a scene closely.

For instance, in *WordPlay Midsummer*, the doubled casting of Hippolyta/Titania and Theseus/Oberon would not be signalled by the text. Students can think about how these characters might be equivalents in interesting ways. Students might also think about Puck's presence in the multiple worlds of the play and how that would make it difficult for an actor to double up in that role. Teachers said that students noticed these doublings. However, the *WordPlay* edition does not explain or comment on the casting choices. When in *WordPlay Romeo and Juliet* actor Myra Lucretia Taylor plays both Lady Montague and the Capulet's Nurse, the actor's appearance in the opening two scenes apparently can cause some confusions for students. At least one teacher used this confusion to prompt students to identify and think about doubling, connecting this aspect of the edition to performance practices in Shakespeare's time (and today). Good class discussions have been reported arising from the question of whether the Tybalt/Paris combination makes sense, and whether both men are equally important to Juliet. Only the lead roles of Macbeth and Lady Macbeth are not doubled in that edition: one teacher said that the class felt this illustrated the couple as being 'together against the world'.

Some students equate editing with 'fixing mistakes'. *WordPlay* supports students learning about editing history by including links to early Shakespeare editions (labelled 'Historical Document'). Pages of *WordPlay Macbeth* that are aligned to a First Folio edition are available from Brandeis University; *Romeo and Juliet* includes links to the British Library's Second Quarto (1599), and *Dream* to its First Quarto (1600). These links might be particularly useful to teachers as they explore the complex history of the publishing of Shakespeare's works with their students and perhaps take on the issues of authorship and authority.

The texts of *WordPlay Shakespeare* editions are sourced from the complete GNU (General Public) licensed versions of the plays, which combine the First Folio of 1623 and the Globe edition of 1866. Students could look to the *WordPlay* foreword to the play, which emphasizes that neither the text nor the performance deletes anything. While acknowledging that most directors choose to cut or condense scenes (for example, removing the musicians who are hanging around after Juliet's faked death as the wedding celebration becomes a funeral), Parker determined that the *WordPlay* edition would not represent a director's cut. There may be 'a few thee/thous exchanged', he insisted, but the performance is 'clean and faithful to the words on the other side of the page'. Each edition makes the gentle boast that it does 'what no book before has done, by bringing together a full and faithful performance of every line of the play with the full text of the play. Not a few scenes. Not the famous soliloquies. The whole play'.

There are sound pedagogical reasons to remind students that the early publications of the plays were as scripts, such as described in detail in Kevin Long and Mary Cristel's 2019 *Bring on the Bard*. One of the provided questions in *WordPlay Romeo and Juliet* (Act 1 Scene 3) supports this approach, asking students to look more closely:

> Stage directions appear in every play you read. Please identify which of the following instructions does not appear on this page:

A. The location of the scene
B. All the characters who will appear in this scene
C. The day of the week on which the scene takes place
D. Stage directions for Lady Capulet, the Nurse, and Juliet

Students can notice that the links *WordPlay* provides are to a Quarto that indicates only entrances. By emphasizing the lack of original stage directions, teachers have reason to remind students that what is supposed to happen on the stage is 'hidden' in the characters' speeches.

2.1.6 Social Learning through Theatre-Based Teaching Approaches

Ambitious teaching taps into the power of social learning, engaging students as group members and building on their heterogeneity. Drama-based practices are a wonderful example of this kind of learning. *WordPlay Shakespeare* was seen as complementing theatre-based practices: one teacher found that *WordPlay* gave students ideas for what to do when they performed a scene, and said it helped them imagine how the actions of a scene might look when not limited to the acting ability (and space) of a classroom. Teachers described integrating *WordPlay* with theatre practices because it is important for students to be 'acting it out so they can understand it'. Another teacher described students using the interactive edition of *Romeo and Juliet* to imagine the (Act 1 Scene 5) party scene and Tybalt's fierce anger in contrast to Capulet's soothing words to keep a fight from breaking out. Students who had access to both *WordPlay* and the (pre-Covid) classroom for enacting scenes told another teacher that experiences that helped them feel Tybalt's thwarted rage made the later fatal street-fighting outburst more understandable.

I do not want to minimize what the pandemic cost teachers, nor to gloss over how mournfully expert teachers spoke of their lost classroom teaching practices: the costumes and swords they usually stocked in their classrooms, and the missed opportunities for students to immerse themselves in the text under the direct guidance of a teacher as director and explicator. Yet *WordPlay*'s support of embodied learning was expressed another way by a teacher who self-described as 'not a drama person'. This teacher found *WordPlay* enabled students to better see how Shakespeare's lines in the famous embedded sonnet (*Romeo and Juliet* Act 1 Scene 5) include 'palm-to-palm' and other stage directions embedded in the text. The argument about whether embodied learning includes watching enactments of texts is an argument for another book.

Several teachers believed students were better able to identify the cues in the text for action and expression because they saw those words enacted: they described their students as 'needing' these visual cues. Teachers contrasted using *WordPlay* with more typically reading the play aloud in class. They appreciated how the production in *WordPlay* offered more information through performance than what classroom actors (students) were typically able to depict. Teachers were impressed with classroom discussions where students were able to identify a character's emotions as indicated in the text (and expressed physically and vocally in the performance): one teacher said that *WordPlay* could be said to help 'imaginatively deprived' kids. If in a 'normal' (non-*WordPlay*) classroom the sequence would be reading aloud, teaching (identifying key ideas), and then going back into the text, one teacher felt the contrast was clear: 'with *WordPlay* they jump to meaning faster'.

2.1.7 Authentic Assessments of Student Learning

WordPlay Shakespeare embeds questions as checks for understanding throughout the scenes. Teachers who used *WordPlay* were able to ask students questions that checked for their understanding rather than for their memorization of what several called 'trivia'. They reported that they had a much better sense of what the students were and were not understanding about the play as they moved through the text, and they credited the embedded questions as well as the performance.

A question from Act 1 Scene 1 of *Macbeth* offers an example of both the tone and the structure of the questions that *WordPlay* includes. Teachers who assign them believe these questions can reinforce students' thinking about the language of the play and their recognition of recurring images.

> Question 1: There are several themes that run through *Macbeth*, one of which is the idea that all that we see is not as it seems, and that there are confusing things that are put in our way to lead us astray. What might suggest that in this brief passage?

A. The reference to one of the witches' familiar spirits
B. The fact that they all leave the stage together
C. The notion that things that seem foul may be beautiful, and vice versa
D. That the air is foggy and filthy, making it hard to see

It seems especially helpful that the *WordPlay* edition eschews labelling passages by simplistic themes and instead uses a question, like in this example, to lead the reader to recognize what such a theme might look like as a written-out statement or thesis.

One group of teachers reported using the built-in questions as exit tickets: when students were working independently through the edition these marked their progress. Teachers also said they created their own guides to accompany *WordPlay*, asking students to track themes or gather quotes, reflecting on what they noticed in the play. In using *WordPlay*, however, they reported they did not need to collect 'lengthy crazy notes' because it was obvious that the students were understanding what they were reading. Instead, one teacher used a 'simple graphic organizer' for students to use to keep track of events and key quotes. Others reported they were able to have their students work together to create mind-maps of the play, full of text-based examples.

Teachers explained that the pandemic had restricted the extensiveness of their writing assignments (such as literary analysis work). Nevertheless, they believed they were seeing students who were more comfortable with finding text evidence: for initial prompts, such as whether Romeo is right in accepting Juliet's ultimatum to get married; and for argumentative work, such as determining who is most responsible for the deaths of Romeo and Juliet. Describing their pre-Covid classrooms, teachers told me that student understanding of a play was typically demonstrated through formal writing, sometimes in conjunction with multiple-choice tests. And they saw, after incorporating *WordPlay*, that when students were given the choice of a text to write about for an exam they chose the Shakespeare play. Other teachers found that, when students were asked to write comparisons (such as between the play, as taught using the *WordPlay* edition, and the Baz Luhrmann production), they were more knowledgeable about the play text in specific ways.

In the online teaching necessitated by Covid, *WordPlay*'s embedded notes and question prompts allowed teachers to move discussions forward even if they did not have the luxury of time to explore as many ideas with their students in their much-restricted synchronous class sessions. One teacher told me it was lucky if a class could cover one key idea in a week and felt grateful that *WordPlay* enabled her students to understand much more than what she was able to cover.

2.2 The Whole Selves of Students

2.2.1 Access to Shakespeare

Students have academic identities sometimes determined by their interest in and ability with schoolwork. Depending on the reading/literacy level of the students, teachers have different expectations for what students will be able to understand about a Shakespeare play. For instance, US teachers will reference 'PreAP kids' as shorthand for those who are believed to be able to go beyond plot and character identification to explore allusions and other more sophisticated literary devices. However, one teacher using *WordPlay*, heard from a specialist that the special education-identified students in the class were 'really digging' *WordPlay*: they were benefitting from the summaries and the opportunity to watch and rewatch different scenes, and their increased depth of understanding was impressive to both teachers.

Teachers using *WordPlay Shakespeare* said they found their students were much more motivated to work through a set of scenes on their own. To these educators, students using *WordPlay* independently improved in both affect and understanding. For many of the teachers I spoke with, the combination of viewing and reading the play meant their students seemed more patient with, and even intrigued by, the opportunity to review, go back, and listen/watch again in order to make sense of the play. In my earlier study, that was exactly what happened with students who had *WordPlay* instead of a printed text.

Teachers welcomed what they felt was faster student understanding through *WordPlay*. They didn't miss what they described as typical 'exhaustion' from teaching Shakespeare. Instead of the teacher playing a recording and spending great effort cajoling 'the ideas out of the kids', teachers found that students reading and viewing *WordPlay* 'have a foundation, and they can get to a line of inquiry [so] fast'. According to several teachers, during teaching online during the pandemic, advanced students were exploring the additional resources as they were largely learning on their own. As one teacher described, 'The ones it helps the most are the motivated or proactive students. They will go and pursue, look at the translation. Watch the play and the reading, go into the glosses.' This is remarkable during the pandemic, this teacher continued, because 'that takes energy. I've gained a new appreciation for how it feels to be 9th graders in front of computers all day long'. As US teachers return to in-person teaching, they may feel more comfortable requiring students of all ability levels to access and explore the materials provided under 'More'.

With whatever combination of instructional strategies to the play they chose, many teachers saw *WordPlay* having an impact on student understanding. They reported that the 'affective barrier', where students are unmotivated to do the work of understanding Shakespeare, 'is lower, and there's more engagement'. Students for instance picked up on a level of humour (including innuendo) that they 'otherwise don't get'. In one school students used *WordPlay Romeo and Juliet* as ninth graders and then *WordPlay Macbeth* the following year. Teachers heard new student confidence, with statements like 'I know I can read it' coming from the students who were veteran users of *WordPlay*.

2.2.2 Identity and Shakespeare's Relevance

There are teaching opportunities that arise using *WordPlay Shakespeare* and its casting (see Figure 4). One teacher told me that students had to 'get over the fact that whoever is acting is just a human' and accept unexpected diversity (in race and gender, for instance) of people in roles. Teachers reported that students commented on the different actors, and teachers believed that students saw themselves in the modernity and diversity of the cast.

WordPlay Shakespeare is an interactive digital edition designed with multiple features that can support ambitious teaching: students can engage in close reading through watching the play performed as well as reading the

Figure 4 *WordPlay Shakespeare*'s diverse casting for *Macbeth*

text, supported by the glosses and other supplementary features for meaning-making. Although the Covid pandemic and its online teaching made many theatre-based classroom practices difficult to adapt to a virtual classroom, teachers reported that they had found ways to engage students with each other and the text. The edition offers teachers tools for meaningfully assessing students' understanding. Teachers also have many opportunities to prompt students to more in-depth critical thinking through comparing the performance of the play with what the text beside it seemed to indicate. *WordPlay Shakespeare* apparently enables students with a wider range of abilities to make sense of the complex language of a play. There is some evidence that the diversity of the casting helps students recognize themselves in the productions. Perhaps the most compelling evidence of how *WordPlay Shakespeare* can support ambitious teaching comes from the ways teachers described watching students make sense of a play, utilizing the tools and gaining more independence.

3 Teaching with *PerformancePlus*: A Case of Theatrical Productions Supporting Meaning-Making

The Stratford Festival (Ontario, Canada) developed *PerformancePlus* as one online dimension of the theatre company's extensive education outreach. The festival has been in the live theatre business with multiple venues since 1953 and, like other theatre companies, strives to attract young people and build an audience. Before the pandemic, the Stratford Festival had hosted thousands of students to matinee performances and hundreds of teachers in workshops and seminars. Its geographical location in Ontario reaches Canadian schools and those in Michigan and New York in the northern United States. The festival's web presence and especially its recorded productions are designed to give its offerings increased national and international prominence.

The festival provides an extensive set of digital resources for teachers, especially those bringing students to performances. Visitors can access 'Stratford Shorts', two-page overviews that introduce and summarize a season's stage offerings, and study guides for students. There are links to workshops and Q&As, Youth Programs, Behind-the Scenes Programs, and 'at the Festival' information for planning trips and participating in drama camps and theatre artist training. The *PerformancePlus* interactive editions are nested under a 'Learn' tab on the Festival's homepage. Each provides a Shakespeare production filmed from the 2014 or later season, a scrolling text that highlights speeches as they are performed, and extensive 'Artistic Insights': video interviews with the director, cast, and creative crew. There are also lesson plans for teaching the play along with the specific production.

Teachers who participate in the festival's professional development workshops and summer institutes experience a combination of theatre work, Shakespeare performance scholarship, and pedagogy, building teacher expertise for collaborating with teaching artists and borrowing from drama-based teaching strategies. The festival's Education Director, by way of the Michigan Members and Teacher Advisory committee, helped me contact individuals to interview about *Performance Plus* at use in classrooms.[21] Some of

---

[21] Thanks to the teachers interviewed about *PerformancePlus*: Natalia Bondar, Lisa Dobbin, Laura Dobsinai, and Lisa Simas.

these teachers had participated in multiple professional development programmes and had a strong history with Stratford performances, bringing students to the theatre and using the study guides and lesson plans. These teachers felt a relationship, even a partnership with the Stratford Festival.

The teachers interviewed felt that *PerformancePlus* editions were a great opportunity for their students. They appreciated how *PerformancePlus* was adapting to Covid realities by including online suggestions for how teachers can 'Tailor *PerformancePlus* to Suit Your Current Learning Mode'. Education Director Lois Adamson reported tracking viewership of their digital resources year over year. The pandemic has had a clear impact: while the festival doesn't know the details about the users or their purposes, in the first half of 2021 alone, more than 60,000 people used *PerformancePlus*.

The teachers appreciated the free access to *PerformancePlus* editions, although they each looked forward to returning to their usual classroom teaching and having the interactive editions to supplement, rather than replace, their instruction.

In the case of *PerformancePlus*, ambitious teaching is supported through the ways students are engaged in authentic academic tasks, particularly related to the many strategies for characterization in a theatrical performance. The recorded performance, coupled with the text, supported teaching that focused on the ways that a text is brought to life through skilful gestures, postures, vocal inflections, attitudes, and more.

3.1 Authentic Academic Engagement

The central feature of the *PerformancePlus* interactive edition is the synched script and performance, which the viewer navigates by starting at each act and scene (see Figure 5).

3.1.1 Synopses and Character Identification.

After a reader selects a scene, the *PerformancePlus* edition offers a straightforward synopsis, with an account of actions, including who appears, and what the characters are talking about. There is minimal explanation of motivation or other context. For instance, Act 5 Scene 1 of *Hamlet* captures characters and actions in sequence and without poetic language or challenging syntax:

Figure 5 A navigation page for *Romeo and Juliet* in *PerformancePlus*. A navigation page for Romeo and Juliet in PerformancePlus. Randy Hughson as Capulet, Gordon Patrick White as Paris and Sara Farb as Juliet in Romeo and Juliet, 2017. Play by William Shakespeare. Directed for the stage by Scott Wentworth. Designed by Christina Poddubiuk. Lighting design by Louise Guinand. Directed for film by Barry Avrich.

> Two gravediggers discuss Ophelia's death and debate her right to a Christian burial in light of her apparent suicide. Hamlet enters with Horatio and banters with one of the gravediggers who unearths two skulls, one of whom belongs to Yorick, a court jester that Hamlet knew as a child. A funeral procession approaches and Hamlet and Horatio conceal themselves only to discover that it is Ophelia's funeral they are witnessing. Hamlet comes forward to reveal his identity and he and Laertes fight. Hamlet declares that his love for Ophelia is greater than Laertes's. Claudius assures Laertes his time for vengeance is near.

There is also a character list for each scene, with a photograph of the actor playing the part and short statements to further remind the reader/viewer who is who. These descriptions appear the same throughout the production, as might be offered in a playbill, rather than updating or changing along with the changing circumstances of the play. Each time Hamlet[22] appears in the character list, he holds a skull and is described as

> the Prince of Denmark and the protagonist. Hamlet is the son of Gertrude and the late King Hamlet. He has returned from his studies at the university in Wittenberg to attend his father's funeral and witness his mother's marriage to his uncle Claudius. His reflective and melancholy nature impedes his ability to avenge his father's murder.

Similarly, the Earl of Gloucester[23] in *King Lear* is described:

> Lear's loyal chief nobleman and father of Edgar and Edmund. His story arc parallels Lear's. Gloucester misjudges both of his sons – he believes ill of Edgar and good of Edmund. He is easily overpowered by Goneril, Regan and Cornwall, but he later comes to a realization of his errors in judgment and shows that he is also capable of great bravery.

Ambitious teaching would remind the reader that these commentaries are potentially arguments, rather than statements of 'facts'. Students could watch for instances where Hamlet is seeking revenge or Gloucester is making mistakes. Reading these descriptions while working through a play for the first time, students can be alerted to characterization and ways the performance depicts Hamlet's nature and Gloucester's judgment. In this way they can avoid thinking that the somewhat reductive character identifications are authoritative. The ambiguity might generate discussion. The 'Artistic Insights' videos (discussed below) offer more nuanced and

---

[22] Actor Jonathan Goad plays Hamlet in this filmed production. As discussed further below, the actors receive opening credits, but are not associated with characters' names except at the end of the production, and if then appearing in the 'Artistic Insights' videos.

[23] Played by actor Scott Wentworth.

complex discussions of the characters and certainly of the broad themes illustrated by the production.

3.1.2 Translations

PerformancePlus editions do not provide a modern English version of the play. The Shakespeare text that is synchronized to the performance includes select words in bold text that students can scroll over for a quick definition in superscript. Multiple teachers particularly appreciated this feature for students who were making sense of the play more independently during the pandemic. In Act 2 Scene 2 for example, Romeo refers to Juliet's eyes that 'twinkle in their spheres' (line 31), and students can mouse over 'sphere' and read that 'stars and planets were thought to be contained in transparent spheres that rotated around the earth'; and that Juliet's eyes would be bright in the 'airy region' refers to 'the sky/galaxy' he is imagining.

In *Macbeth*'s Act 2 Scene 3 Porter's monologue, the glosses offer literal as well as suggestive explanations of bawdy idioms. For instance, 'stealing out of a French hose' (line 14) is glossed as 'Stealing cloth while in the process of making pants/being too lecherous and letting his penis steal too often out of his pants (French hose).' And explains that 'tailors were often viewed as lustful'. Similarly 'roast your goose' (line 15) is explained as 'heat up your tailor's iron/ have sex with your prostitute', and notes that *goose* is 'slang for prostitute'.

As an interactive edition, *PerformancePlus* emphasizes how the work of acting creates characters, and that production decisions (costuming, lighting, and staging) support specific characterizations. It also offers frequent reminders to the student that the text is the foundation of their collaborative theatre-making work. In this way teachers can lead students to think more carefully about characterization as it is indicated in what they are reading. Teachers reported that what students noticed, and how they talked about the characters as portrayed in the production, often offered teachable moments, opportunities for teachers to help students articulate their expectations for a character. Sometimes these expectations included stereotypes that could interfere with their understanding of a particular production. For instance, students in one classroom using *PerformancePlus* asked, 'How old is Juliet supposed to be, anyway?' This was more than just questioning a casting decision: it also got at the actor's portrayal. It may be that everyone 'knows' that Juliet is almost fourteen, but what really needed discussing was how a person moves in the awkwardness of adolescence. The teacher was able to ask, what human actions reveal youth? This conversation then led to one student describing the paralysis of self-consciousness, and the students talking about the influences of community (and school) norms. *PerformancePlus* offered a great opening for discussing what makes a characterization compelling. Students could also see gestures and physical attitudes an actor takes while a character is not speaking, or is perhaps not even the centre of a given scene. These are details of portrayal that are rarely brought to classroom read-alouds or enactments.

3.1.3 Glosses and Notes on the Text

The 'Artistic Insight' videos embedded in the *PerformancePlus* interactive edition offer important additional ideas about characterization, especially as contributing to the design and intention of a specific production. These videos are 3- to 5-minute interviews focused on a single topic, a strategy that makes it easy for teachers to sample and share individual selections in support of their teaching goals or in answer to student questions. Actors from each production are interviewed about the character they are portraying, and they explain motivation, desires, and internal reasoning, often quoting from their lines or describing specific key scenes. As an example, Krystin Pellerin (playing Lady Macbeth) describes her character as having 'a part of her that's broken; she's lost her child . . . she will do anything to feel fulfilled or complete'. Pellerin explains that this is why Lady Macbeth is open to the 'dark side' of what the weird sisters prophesy.

The lesson plans provided with the different *PerformancePlus* editions offer useful questions for spurring reflection on the intersections of character and plot points, including statements for students to debate, such as:

- Juliet should marry Paris
- Mercutio is a superior swordsman to Tybalt
- Romeo and Juliet's love is just infatuation
- Mercutio and the Nurse are unnecessary characters in the play
- Friar Laurence does more harm than good

Similarly the *Hamlet* edition offers 'Post Act 5 Discussion Points' that include wide-ranging considerations, such as:

- What role do women play in *Hamlet*?
- How do the issues present in *Hamlet* reflect our society today?
- Discuss Hamlet's love for Ophelia – was it genuine or not?
- Is *Hamlet* a revenge play?
- Would Hamlet have made a good ruler?

The wide-ranging 'Artistic Insight' videos support the viewer's understanding of the text as a basis for action. The range of topics and organization of these commentaries varies by edition. *King Lear*'s 'Artistic Insight' videos are broken up by acts and describe 'General Themes' and separately 'Blindness' and 'Disguise'; Act 3 videos highlight staging and design, with 'The Storm' and 'Costuming'. Other videos are focused on potential student questions. *Hamlet* includes a video entitled 'Advice to Students Studying Shakespeare'. In it one actor exhorts students to 'be patient' because the 'impenetrable language' pays off eventually. Another actor urges anyone to 'speak it out loud' because of the rhythm that helps to make the meaning, while a third says 'cast out fear' because 'it's your language'. A final speaker urges students to have fun with the language and to embrace 'failure' because there is no one right way – 'anyway you can come at this and enjoy it, is fantastic'. Actor Jonathan Goad, who plays Hamlet, has an entire menu of videos discussing topics from 'Hamlet and His Family Dynamics' to 'Hamlet's Fatal Flaw'.

Teaching a play using *PerformancePlus* invites students into critical conversations about meaning communicated with both language and action. Students in one classroom discussed the degree to which Lady Macbeth's ambition was portrayed as sexualized, and what other textual evidence there was for the 'hot' performance of the relationship between the Macbeths. The interviewed teachers believed that student analysis was elevated by their use of *PerformancePlus*, that students felt more confident in their critical voices. They seemed to feel invited to dive into the play in academically intensive ways.

3.1.4 Text and Performance Combined

PerformancePlus gives students a clear picture of what was happening on the stage and an easy way to connect it to the script. Enabling students to view a performance while reading a text at the same time took 'some of the work off our plates', in the words of one teacher. Teachers said that as a result there was much in the play that 'didn't have to be explained'. Teachers who used *PerformancePlus* in face-to-face teaching appreciated being able to isolate and hone in on particular moments in the text, the acting, and the action. That said, another teacher who described the set-up of the edition as 'fantastic' for classroom projection wished it were possible to 'run the whole thing in its entirety' for students.

Teachers appreciated how the Stratford Festival's staging consistently emphasizes that Shakespeare created a play without elaborate scenery or many special effects. As a result, students could recognize the performances as demonstrating some of the constraints Shakespeare's time gave him as a playwright, and thus an explanation for 'why there's so much imagery in the language'. One teacher using *PerformancePlus* appreciated how an actor's body language and voice expressiveness enabled students to find complex speeches meaningful. In addition, the embedded performance in the edition meant that students had an illustration of what an 'aside' looks like, and could better understand how the staging of soliloquys and monologues would make it clear that no one else on the stage was hearing a particular speech. One teacher described how students paid attention to the banquet scene in *Macbeth*, watching the physical movement, the turn of attention, as well as noting the change in the tone of voice, when Macbeth moves from speaking to Lady Macbeth to addressing a servant. Teachers did not feel they needed to point out each one of these moments, although they would highlight some, early, in order to attune students to the move from page to stage. Students gained deepened, more nuanced understandings, according to teachers: they see 'more than fear', for instance, they see fear 'coupled with disbelief'. In another case students see 'not just anger, but arrogance and disrespect'.

One student commented on *PerformancePlus Romeo and Juliet* that Romeo was 'spending a lot of time on the floor of the stage', and the teacher answered, 'Yes, and why do you think that's being done?' Students reading and viewing Act 2 Scene 2 became more conscious of how often Romeo was addressing the sky, Juliet's balcony, heaven, and fate, and how this was reinforced by his physical stance.

Lesson plans provided with the *PerformancePlus Lear* edition can support teachers as they guide students in character analysis. For instance, *King Lear's* 'Charting the Character Arc' references Edmund and Edgar, the half-brothers, but its questions are applicable for many characters. These include:

- Does the character start with a certain viewpoint at the beginning and change over the course of the play?
- Did the character undergo personal growth and development?

One teacher interviewed pointed out that *PerformancePlus* gave students the ability to navigate 'backwards' in the play, through the interactive edition (asking, for instance, 'how did she act the first time we saw her?'). As a result, students could better note a character's development over time. Teachers could ask students where *Romeo and Juliet* turned from comedy to tragedy, and how did they know; using *PerformancePlus* enabled students to see the change in the performance as well as read the lines that indicated it.

Ambitious teaching can prepare students to focus on more than what happens next. Teachers recognized that even as the performance enabled students to 'just watch what the actors do', this alone would not reveal *why* an actor was making specific choices. Teaching (or at least reading) was still required for students to pay close attention to the connections between language (the text) and actions, and how Shakespeare was cueing the actors through what he had them say.

Because many teachers include comparative film clips of scenes, they found it was important for students to remember *PerformancePlus* incorporates a *recorded* stage production. The director who is interviewed is the one who created the theatre event, not who filmed it. The filming of the play is not much discussed in these editions, even though it is sophisticated. The reader experiences the video as if from the perspective of the audience, and additional camera work provides close-ups and some reaction shots. For instance, in Act 2 Scene 2 when Romeo wishes to be 'a glove upon that hand / That I might touch that cheek' the reader is hearing Romeo speak but seeing Juliet, hand on her cheek, looking out into the night. Because the reader / viewer shares the point of view with Romeo, the shot communicates how he would touch Juliet's face if he could (see Figure 6).

Figure 6 The filmed production of Romeo and Juliet in PerformancePlus and its use of camera angles. Sara Farb as Juliet in Romeo and Juliet, 2017. Play by William Shakespeare. Directed for the stage by Scott Wentworth. Designed by Christina Poddubiuk. Lighting design by Louise Guinand. Directed for film by Barry Avrich

In a *PerformancePlus* video following Act 5 in *Lear*, Colm Feore discusses acting on the Festival stage when the performance is being recorded. He describes how his acting is influenced by the knowledge of where the different cameras are and what they will capture. 'When we film these, we bring ten cameras in'. he says, and goes on to explain that he is playing to both the audience and the cameras and does things differently, 'So that we don't overdo for film what we're doing for stage'. Stephen Ouimette (who plays the Fool) offers a contrasting opinion. He claims that the cameras 'were unseen to us' because of where they are positioned. Ouimette further reflects on the fact that the lighting is so good, in modern theatre, that actors don't need much make-up, and the 'style of acting has changed, it's come down from a slightly more bombastic, loud, shouty style of acting to a more conversational tone'. As a result he believes there is less of a difference between stage and film. Jonathan Goad, playing Kent, says that on stage an actor is responsible for both 'the wide shot and the intimate shot', whereas the camera is only representing one perspective. Teachers can use this video (whether or not they are studying *Lear*) to open a discussion of the impact of a camera angle, and the decisions that are made in *PerformancePlus* and in all filming.

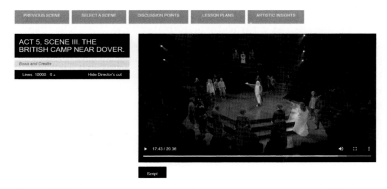

Figure 7 The viewer sees the audience's ovation at the conclusion of King Lear in PerformancePlus. Colm Feore as King Lear with the full cast in King Lear, 2014. Play by William Shakespeare. Directed for the stage by Antoni Cimolino. Designed by Eo Sharp. Lighting design by Michael Walton. Directed for film by Barry Avrich

Although the teachers interviewed only mentioned this quality in passing, the presence of the audience in the *PerformancePlus* editions is a further opportunity to encourage students to think about how that presence influences one's perception of the play.[24] There is a sometimes-visible audience, whose laughter often seems knowing and appreciative. Ambitious teaching can draw student attention to it: why does *PerformancePlus* include the audience? What is being communicated about theatre and how they might react to it? Students can see the standing ovation given to the *Hamlet* production, and the particularly loud ovation for Colm Feore as Lear: indeed, every production closes with a dark stage that is quickly roared to life by the audience, and all the actors take well-choreographed bows before there are traditional film credits (see Figure 7).

---

[24] Margaret Jane Kidnie names this perspective *visible spectatorship* in her chapter on the Stratford Festival in *Shakespeare and the 'Live' Theater Broadcast Experience* (Aebischer, Greenhaigh, and Osborne 2018).

In its current design, a teacher who wants to emphasize the production in *PerformancePlus* as a particular performance faces a few challenges. Cast lists take some work to find (I recommend screenshots from the credits at the end of the film). The 'Artistic Insight' videos do identify actor and character when playing, but this information might be incorporated with the titles of the videos. There are many demands on a theatre company's time, and of course competing priorities. But a few more aids/ supplements to the production could enhance, even maximize teacher use of *PerformancePlus* interactive edition as a strategy (for students) to not only understand a Shakespeare play more deeply but also to be guided in thinking about the work of making theatre.

Teachers also described selectively incorporating other production versions of a given play, including clips from key scenes, to heighten the students' sense of what was possible. When using other film clips, one teacher said, she made *PerformancePlus* the anchor, because of the convenient availability of the text. This teacher described students comparing *Romeo and Juliet* balcony scenes, for instance, responding to simple prompts ('What made that something you connected with?' or 'What was off-putting?') and learning to articulate their ideas using the terminology of theatre and film. Teachers suggested the platform might itself include 'alternative' production clips, from other productions of the same plays at the Stratford Festival and possibly from 'sister institutions' like the Royal Shakespeare Company and Shakespeare's Globe. The teachers emphasized that there was nothing like comparing film clips of specific scenes for demonstrating to students that no performance is ever definitive.

3.1.5 Critical Thinking about Intentions and Art Making

In *PerformancePlus* the play on stage is central, and the 'Plus' provides insights into the text by revealing the perspectives of the workers creating theatre: actors, designers, and directors. Lois Adamson, Stratford Festival's Director of Education, described *PerformancePlus* as preserving something of the ephemeral magic of live theatre for students to experience, and yet at the same time, Adamson told me the goal is also to 'kill the magic' by revealing the work of making the art. She sees the 'Artistic Insight' videos, for instance, as inviting people into the process.

By highlighting the directorial vision, the actors' choices in creating their roles, the set designs, costuming, and more, the purpose is to communicate that *this is all created*. The message, to young readers especially, is that nothing 'just happens' in theatre. Adamson emphasized that it is an important pedagogical stance that students themselves need to feel they have a contribution to make, rather than feeling that they are receiving something that just 'is'.

To the teachers interviewed, using *PerformancePlus* meant that students could consider a play and its interpretation through production. Students have access to the Director's choices in staging, costuming, and sound. They can observe how an actor creates a character and the skills needed to convincingly perform a role. Students can see not only the original Shakespeare text but also what lines have been cut. Students can also see the text performed in unexpected ways. Students could consider the reasons why, after the Prologue, the *Romeo and Juliet* production offered a soundscape of words. No one was seen speaking lines like 'A dog of the house of Montague', and yet in this production the words (recorded and played while the characters on stage are not speaking) are in the air of Verona. Then one man's spoken 'Do you bite your thumb at us, sir' begins the escalation towards the street fight.

One of the benefits of emphasizing performance as a series of decisions, as one teacher explained, is that students otherwise think of Shakespeare as 'up there, in the untouchable canon'. Students can realize instead that 'It's not this thing that can never be changed' as they interact with the play. The teacher's role here is important, reminding students that they are witnessing one production, one coherent interpretation reinforced from director to designers to actors.

PerformancePlus actors are named along with their roles in the characterization-oriented videos. The 'Artistic Insights' could do more to frame the actor's answers as from *this* production. Otherwise, an actor's authority from performing a role might discourage students from question and critique. The videos might inadvertently encourage the viewer to interpret the play as fully 'explained', and a teacher's guide could help an ambitious educator point out or highlight even more of the interpretive decisions.

3.1.6 Social Learning through Theatre-Based
Teaching Approaches

Given that many professional development programmes at the Stratford Festival prepare teachers to work with teaching artists and offer adaptations of theatre exercises and rehearsal room activities to use in their classrooms, *PerformancePlus* may seem a counterintuitive educational endeavour. Some Shakespeare educators dismiss filmed productions out of the belief that students need to speak the lines in order to make meaning of them. The Stratford Festival takes a different path, incorporating examples and guides for integrating theatre-based activities into classrooms in *PerformancePlus*. According to Lois Adamson, *PerformancePlus*, when compared to just reading the text, is not a passive exercise: students 'see it embodied' and hear Shakespeare enacted. The edition works to bridge from virtual consumption of the play to active learning by incorporating exercises and demonstrations by teaching artists as well as the insights from directors and actors.

To support on-your-feet approaches, *PerformancePlus* provides a video of teaching artist Luisa Appolloni leading an activity for Act 3 *Macbeth*, a Character Frieze (Living Sculptures) exercise (see Figure 8). In another, students have memorized different lines from *Hamlet*, and they are tapped on their shoulder to deliver a favourite excerpt. There are also examples of student teams creating and performing choral work. The short videos are meant to support teachers carrying out this kind of active work, although only the ones with *The Tempest* show 'normal' classrooms per se, while others film students in a spacious studio.

Another teacher referenced the usefulness of 'status' exercises that draw from theatre games and using these to help students see how Capulet was 'switching personalities' when he talked to Tybalt, and then the servants and other guests in Act 1 Scene 5 of *Romeo and Juliet*. Other theatre-based lessons plans linked to both the *Hamlet* and *Romeo and Juliet* *PerformancePlus* editions include an activity reminiscent of the Cecily Berry 'walking the punctuation' exercise, where students are encouraged to experience how a character physically acts while making a decision or determining a course of action. In this lesson, students are reading aloud and they switch speakers whenever there is a punctuation mark in the text,

Figure 8 Actor Andre Sills, a Stratford Festival teaching artist, works with students on staging the storm in *The Tempest*

emphasizing changes in perspective on a problem. One teacher interviewed combined an active reading of the play with watching *PerformancePlus*, and students recognized 'their' lines. Students told her 'I never heard the line that way'. Students gained ideas about reading (acting) with tone; they caught the humour and imagined 'Shakespeare characters that banter like real humans' through these exercises. These teachers' classrooms counter the idea that interactive editions necessarily mean passive student consumption of plays, but ambitious teaching is required.

The teachers interviewed who had experienced professional development through the Stratford Festival were especially committed to student learning through classroom enactments and other theatre-based exercises, and they were feeling the loss of these because of Covid-19 and distance teaching. As I interviewed them in their classrooms (on Zoom), the teachers pointed out how their rooms were filled with props and materials for impromptu staging and costuming, none of which could be used. They said they struggled to create online experiences, for instance, that could be as meaningful as the choral readings that were regularly part of their practice.

3.2 The Whole Selves of Students

3.2.1 Identity and Shakespeare's Relevance

Lois Adamson, the Stratford's Director of Education, describes *PerformancePlus* as offering not just a play, but also a reflection of our time in culture and history. Adamson wants teachers and students to understand, through *PerformancePlus*, that there is no one right way to perform or present a Shakespeare play. Adamson described the *PerformancePlus* project as intended to capture the Shakespeare canon in a Canadian voice for students. For Adamson, this also meant that the resources provided for studying the plays would emphasize not just the works, but also the ways that the productions are responsive to contemporary times. There is a lesson, for instance, in the *PerformancePlus Romeo and Juliet* entitled 'Preventing Teen Suicide' that focuses on Juliet's stress, and on warning signs, and that considers what strategies, and by whom, could have prevented the characters' deaths. This material draws from more than the play and connects to advice and further resources from the Canadian Mental Health Association.

PerformancePlus and the Stratford Festival more broadly are engaged in embracing the moment in terms of anti-racism and promoting increased social opportunity and equity, and this despite the closures and cancellations from the Covid pandemic. It is fair to describe the casting in *PerformancePlus* productions as colour-blind, although the artists interviewed make multiple references to the Stratford casts intentionally representing all of Canada. The casting of the 2016 production of *Macbeth* includes Lady Macduff played by Sarah Afful, who is Black (see Figure 9), and in that production 'Young Macduff' is a white child, although Michael Blake, as Macduff, is Black (see Figure 10). Students might be encouraged to think about whether the Black couple is cast as a moral centre for the play.

PerformancePlus editions have been evolving throughout the pandemic, including the creation of *Tempest* and *Othello* plays in the series that offer only three scenes in side-by-side text and performance but still include many 'Artistic Insight' videos. Both are very interesting theatrical productions, and their truncated editions suggest many sites for ambitious teaching. The *PerformancePlus Tempest*, in which Martha Henry plays a female Prospero, is

Figure 9 Sarah Afful as Lady Macduff, Oliver Neudorf as Young Macduff and David Collins as Ross in Macbeth, 2016. Play by William Shakespeare. Directed for the stage by Antoni Cimolino. Designed by Julie Fox. Lighting design by Michael Walton. Directed for film by Barry Avrich

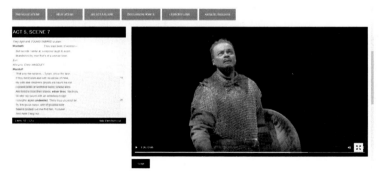

Figure 10 Michael Blake as Macduff in Macbeth, 2016. Play by William Shakespeare. Directed for the stage by Antoni Cimolino. Designed by Julie Fox. Lighting design by Michael Walton. Directed for film by Barry Avrich

a production that Artistic Director Antoni Cimolino describes as inspired by Queen Elizabeth I and criticism the monarch received at the end of her life that she was insufficiently aggressive against England's foes. In her interview Martha Henry seems somewhat bemused by having played Miranda years ago at the beginning of her career at Stratford when she says, 'I now discover it's a play about a woman.' After Act 5, one question set includes two particularly relevant queries. 'Prospero was originally written as a male character. Does having a woman playing the part of Prospero change your perspective about the character and her motivations?' Students are also asked to discuss Caliban. 'Is he a hero, villain, or morally ambiguous? In what ways is he impacted by colonization?' There is no reference to Caliban being played by a Black actor (Michael Blake).

Blake also plays *Othello* in the most recently (spring 2021) available *PerformancePlus* edition. The marquee (landing page) highlights that the production was praised as 'electrifying from start to finish', although this *PerformancePlus* edition has only three scenes offered as paired text/performance. There are multiple lesson plans and video interviews, and in large part the supporting materials are focused on race, misogyny, and power. Actors appear to take a lead in making statements about the play and explaining 'to what end do we programme and perform this play today'. The *PerformancePlus Othello* offers 'Resources on Shakespeare, Othello, and Antiracism' and an exercise on 'Racism, White Supremacy, and Patriarchy' that is designed to be used during multiple class sessions focused on Act 1 scene 3. The materials include definitions of words like *code-switching* and *misogyny*, *gender equity* and *racism*, and point to different 'Artistic Insight' videos where actors discuss character relationships. Elsewhere on the website, the Stratford Festival makes clear statements about inclusion and anti-racism and social justice.

Here the author must admit to being a passionate fan of the Canadian Broadcasting Company's television series *Slings and Arrows*, depicting a theatre festival (purported to be loosely based on the Stratford Festival) and its three seasons producing Shakespeare plays. In its third *Lear*-focused season, colour-blind casting is depicted, and commented on. William Hutt plays an aging white actor, Charles Kingman, who plays Lear. He directly and caustically comments on the colour-blind casting as the part of Goneril, his daughter, is played by a Black woman. Francesca T. Royster writes, 'the show makes him the voice of conservatism and elitism of past generations'.[25] It is possible that new *PerformancePlus* materials could include explanations for how the casting strives to be colour-conscious, for instance.

3.2.2 Access to Shakespeare

One teacher interviewed not only noted what students gained by working with the *PerformancePlus* edition to make meaning, but also wondered why schools (or English departments) were not rolling out this edition to all of the students. In other words, given a population of at-risk students, supposedly less likely to be successful with Shakespeare, this teacher couldn't understand why every teacher wasn't utilizing this edition as part of their instruction. While not wanting to 'put down' what other teachers were doing, this teacher was dismayed that the edition was not in wider use where there were many students who were English language learners, especially.

One teacher emphasized that teachers and teaching artists and actors (and productions such as those in *PerformancePlus*) all help students understand the necessity of puzzling out lines, because there is no single answer. The interactive edition helps students not be afraid that they 'don't know the answers' as to why an actor is saying or doing a particular thing. As a result, they become more confident with their own interpretations, willing to share their ideas and opinions. Teachers using *PerformancePlus* report that students say Shakespeare plays are 'a lot less boring' and 'easier'. Shakespeare as an author is no longer so 'upper crust', and is more approachable.

Of the three editions discussed in this Element, *PerformancePlus* is the one that teachers expressed the most loyalty to, in that they were the most unhappy with other teachers who have not yet adopted it. Some of these teachers seemed like those I know from the Folger Library's Teaching Shakespeare Institute: they know their transformed teaching practices are having an important impact on students. Teaching Shakespeare during the Covid pandemic was thwarting a lot of their opportunities to use their accustomed and accomplished approaches for teaching, and *PerformancePlus* gave them a useful substitute tool for their in-person classroom teaching.

[25] For a terrific discussion of this season and the whiteness of the Burbage Theater festival, see Royster (2011).

4 Teaching with *myShakespeare*: A Case of Starting Meaningful Conversations

Paradigm Education's *myShakespeare*, an interactive edition hosted on a freely available website, began as a collaboration among educator scholars at Stanford University who shared a passion for both literature and filmmaking. Their primary goal was providing students the resources needed to have detailed, meaningful discussions about Shakespeare plays as literature, as cultural artefacts, and as commentaries on today. Each *myShakespeare* interactive edition[26] includes the full text, with interline glosses that the reader can choose to turn off. Clicking on icons enables the entire play to be heard read aloud, speech-by-speech synched to the text. Icons also open video performances of selected passages in a pop-up window that reveals one or more actors, typically facing the camera, delivering the lines and to some extent interacting. Each play in the edition varies in its assortment of features beyond the central text. But links at the end of almost every scene lead to interviews with one or more of the characters (played by actors) from that scene, with questions asked by a twenty-first-century host.

Greg Watkins is co-director as well as head writer and producer, and his background mirrors that of others on the *myShakespeare* team. These are not formal Shakespeare scholars but rather people dedicated to the humanities, film, and education and holding a wide range of formal degrees from prestigious places: Renaissance people. Richard Clark, also co-director, funds the work, and Sally Treanor works full-time developing teaching materials and the website. They aided me in identifying teachers to interview about *myShakespeare*.[27] In addition to praising *myShakespeare* for being a free resource, these teachers

---

[26] The *myShakespeare* website currently includes *myHamlet*, *myMacbeth*, *myRomeo and Juliet*, *myJulius Caesar*, *myTaming of the Shrew*, and *myMidsummer Night's Dream*.

[27] Many thanks to teachers Leonard Aguilar, Jennifer Black, Natalia Bondar, Rita DaFonseca, Christine Garrity, Anjali Nirmalan, and Ronald 'Tommy' Thibideaux Jr.

repeatedly mentioned the readily available technical support. Greg Watkins and the *myShakespeare* team regularly showcase the features of the platform and brainstorm with teachers about ways to improve the usefulness of the edition for classroom settings. They spent hours meeting with secondary teachers at national NCTE conferences and in addition have appeared at SXSW Education and on digital panels for the Shakespeare Association of America and the World Shakespeare Conference.

During the spring of 2021 the *myShakespeare* site reached almost 300,000 weekly visits, a 100 per cent increase likely due to pandemic teaching. Searching for a way to teach *Julius Caesar*, one teacher found *myShakespeare* through the recommendation of a colleague in a professional development network. Not only did *myShakespeare* seem like an amazing solution for the online teaching situation: it was also free.

As an interactive platform, *myShakespeare* suggests an order for navigating the edition, but the hyperlinks allow the reader to click easily to anywhere in any sequence. While the options are a challenge to describe in a linear text, there are consistent features to explore. Some navigational aids in the *myShakespeare* edition are particularly useful for teachers. There is a 'Direct Links to Media' option that provides a central list and links to all of the short films. The resources are abundant. Act 1 of m*yHamlet* offers three performance videos, four interview videos, and seventy-five animated notes. Act 1 of *myRomeo and Juliet* includes fifteen performance videos, seven interviews, and thirteen notes. In most cases there are also transcripts of the interviews included with the link. While the editions do not list publication dates, they are regularly updated with new features, especially the 'notebook' feature added to support writing assignments with *myShakespeare*.

In the case of *myShakespeare*, teachers who are drawn to this interactive edition seem to be those who want their students to access the rhetorical and intellectual heart of the plays. Their classroom instruction may be less focused on analysis of performances because they are ambitious to get a lot of fundamental information established so that students are ready for rich dialogue about the play and what it means to them.

4.1 Authentic Academic Engagement.

One powerful, if probably unexpected, way that the *myShakespeare* edition encourages academic engagement is through its 'Series Hosts', modern-day characters who are integral to each edition as guides, interviewers, and at times interpreters. The hosts model academic engagement. Arguably they are enacting a goofy approximation of ambitious teaching: modelling engagement, learning in collaboration with others, and even authentically assessing their progress as they seek to understand what is happening and why.

The Series Hosts characters are played by Jeremy Sabol (as Ralph Holinshed), who appears throughout the series, as well Carrie Paff (as Sarah Siddons), Safiya Fredericks (as 'Servilia' and 'Davina' and 'Sofia', depending on the work), and Shannon Tyo conducts interviews in *myMidsummer Night's Dream* as 'Athena'. A careful reader (perhaps prompted by ambitious teaching) can deduce the rules governing the host's engagement with the action of the play. During the interviews, only the host knows fully what has happened so far – like the reader. The characters know only the scenes in which they appear. The hosts introduce themselves and describe their interviews as intended to be 'enlightening and entertaining' and explain that the interviews are of 'characters brought to life' from Shakespeare plays.

Typically the hosts interview the characters in a bare studio around a table, although in *myHamlet* Sarah is 'on the scene' and shown on a stage where theatre is happening (See Video 4). This is the only play in the edition where the interview acknowledges a performance – in the rest, what is happening is in a kind of alternate reality. For instance, when Athena joins Ralph in *myMidsummer Night's Dream*, she conducts on-the-scene interviews with Theseus. Theseus assumes Athena is an entertainment reporter covering his upcoming celebrity wedding. Similarly the Hostess character interviewed about the Act 1 Scene 1 framing story to *myTaming of the Shrew* believes she is taking part in some courtroom drama. The role of the Series Hosts in *myShakespeare* is discussed at length below. Ambitious teaching might encourage students to think like the hosts, to imagine the questions that they want answered in each scene.

Video 4 *myShakespeare*'s on-the-scene interview about Ophelia. Video file is available at www.cambridge.org/turchi

4.1.1 Synopses and Character Identification

The *myShakespeare* digital edition includes scene synopses, available as text and/or animated short films. Readers have the option of watching some of the animated synopses as a single film, but these films are also divided up and accessible by icon at the beginning of each scene. The animated synopses for *myTaming of the Shrew* show the action taking place on a stage, which underscores the edition's depiction of, and emphasis on, the introductory frame of the play (See Video 5). *Shrew* is a performance within a performance, an elaborate joke played on Christopher Sly, a drunken ne'er-do-well.

The text synopsis for Act 4 Scene 1 of *myTaming of the Shrew* includes this hint to the reader: 'It will help to appreciate the humour in this scene if you imagine that the actor playing Grumio is rather small, which was the case at Shakespeare's Globe Theatre.' This is one of the rare cases where the synopsis includes a direct advice on how to understand or interpret the scene.

Video 5 An animated synopsis for *myTaming of the Shrew*. Video file is available at www.cambridge.org/turchi

In addition to the synopses, readers can consult other icons for video options that provide interpretations or perspectives on what is happening. There are summarizing songs in *myHamlet*, and other videos in that play show head shots of the actors as their relationships are diagrammed (narrated by one of the Series Hosts). Ralph and Davina, hosting *myMacbeth*, narrate an explanatory video just after Act 3 Scene 3:

DAVINA: Yes, they managed to kill Banquo. Oh, dear. It's quite
           gruesome, in fact. And let's see – in all of the commotion,
           his son, Fleance escapes.
RALPH: Oh, wow. Fleance escapes. Nice. But wait, that's kind of
           a big deal. I mean, Macbeth knows that he's got to kill
           Fleance if he wants to prove the witches wrong.

Readers who need help identifying characters can use the interviews, where the hosts always remind the viewer of who is who. Within the platform for each play, the cast lists include not only headshots of the actors but often production photos of them as the character in costume. 'Who's Who in Rome' is an animated film to accompany *my Julius Caesar*, and the cartoon characters illustrate the physical features of the respective members of the live cast.

4.1.2 Translations

The 'pop up' translations into modern English provided by *my Shakespeare* supplement the single-word interline definitions in the play text. To illustrate this, consider Petruchio's Act 2 Scene 1 scheme against Kate's sanity in *my Taming of the Shrew*:

> Say that she rail, why then I'll tell her plain
> She sings as sweetly as a nightingale:
> Say that she frown, I'll say she looks as clear 170
> As morning roses newly washed with dew:
> Say she be mute and will not speak a word,
> Then I'll commend her volubility,
> And say she uttereth piercing eloquence:
> If she do bid me pack, I'll give her thanks,
> As though she bid me stay by her a week:
> If she deny to wed, I'll crave the day
> When I shall ask the banns and when be married.

my Shakespeare glosses these words within this text:

> 167 rail – yell
> 172 volubility – fluency
> 174 pack – leave
> 176 crave – request
> 177 ask the banns – make the announcement

And then provides this modern translation:

> If she yells at me, I'll tell her she sings as sweetly as a nightingale. If she frowns, I'll say she looks as serene as roses washed by the morning dew. If she's mute and won't say a word, I'll compliment her talkativeness, her moving

> eloquence. If she sends me packing, I'll thank her as if she'd
> asked me to stay with her for a week. If she says she won't
> marry me, I'll ask her when we should make our marriage
> announcement, and when the wedding will be.

The *myShakespeare* team describes these as 'plain-English' translations
and uses undergraduate students to help create them. This *myHamlet*
translation further highlights the choices made to keep the syntax but
lose the verse:

> To live, or not to live: that is the question. Is it more
> noble to put up with all the difficulties that fate throws our
> way, or to fight against them, and, in fighting them, put an
> end to everything? Death is like sleeping, that's all.
> A kind of sleep that ends the countless heartaches and
> sufferings that are part of life – now that's something to
> be desired. To die, to sleep – and during this sleep, maybe
> we dream.

In a sense, the interviews with the characters also provide translations as the
conversation interpolates conversational language with the original language of the play. Early in *myTaming of the Shrew*, the Hostess character is
startled, even annoyed that she needs to explain so much. In her interview
that accompanies the introductory scene she asks Ralph, 'Are we going to
have to explain every word we say? Because I don't have time for that.'
Ralph also is having trouble making sense of what Duncan is saying in Act 1
Scene 6 of *myMacbeth*, so he inquires:

RALPH: . . . you've all just arrived at the Macbeth castle. And the
              first thing you notice is, well, how lovely it seems. Tell us
              what you say there.
DUNCAN: This castle hath a pleasant seat, the air –
RALPH: I'm sorry. Pleasant seat?
DUNCAN: You know, the whole setup. It's just nice, in general.
RALPH: Oh. Got it. Sorry to interrupt.

4.1.3 Glosses and Notes on the Text

Each play in the edition includes what is positioned as introductory material, animated films such as 'Elizabethan Theatre' or 'Shakespeare's Life' and (for *myJulius Caesar*) 'The Roman Republic'. There are scene synopses at the top of each page, either short texts in a casual register ('Here's what's happening ... ') or a narrated animated presentation that incorporates Shakespeare's lines while capturing key characters and actions. In addition to interline glosses, for every scene there are multiple icons in the margins of the play that the reader can choose to click on, each leading to presentations that annotate the text. These include options labelled as 'Word Nerd', videos which discuss etymology and usage; and others that are explanations of folklore or Biblical allusions, historical references, and Shakespeare's word play. There are invitations to the reader labelled 'Dig Deeper', that analyse thematic elements and sometimes incorporate perspectives from critical scholars. For some of the plays in the interactive edition there are also performances of semi-serious songs summarizing the play's action up to a specific point, and interspersed as well are advertisements, parody commercials for spot remover (*myMacbeth*) and the University of Wittenberg (*myHamlet* (see Video 6)).

The Series hosts pay attention to what's important and make sure the viewer recognizes the key moments and important facts about what is happening. The interviews they conduct at the end of almost every scene effectively review the scene with one or more characters who answer questions in a blend of modern English and phrases from the play text. Typically, the interviews are longer than the given scene: these are less about summarizing and more about seeking to understand. The Series Hosts model a casually investigative stance. By interviewing the characters (rather than the actors about the roles they play), these hosts are unique allies for meaning-making. Their role implicitly suggests *If you could be there (in the play) asking questions, this is what you'd want to know*. They refer to their notes to ask characters about specific lines and review the sequence of events with them. They frequently read to the character about what is happening using direct passages from the text (and thus clarifying it for the reader). The hosts do not make any reference to what will happen next

Video 6 *myHamlet*'s advertisement for the University of Wittenberg. Video file is available at www.cambridge.org/turchi

(what they may know from other characters in other scenes), and so they further the reader/viewer's sense of dramatic irony.

While the hosts rarely break the play's immediate constraints during the interviews, when they also serve as narrators for the other animated explanatory films, they offer information and insight that they would not share with the characters. Early in *myHamlet* they urge the reader to wonder why Hamlet has not been named King of Denmark after the death of his father. The hosts also voice the 'Word Nerd' and other short videos about language and highlighted features in the text, comparing modern understanding and usage to what was likely meant at the time of a given play (when they occasionally do this in the interviews, it usually exasperates the character). In these features, a reader might have some aspect of the play's plot 'spoiled', but viewers who already know even the broad outline of a play will find their understanding enhanced.

Students see the hosts work to avoid 'spoilers'. Ralph and Sarah offer a jaunty start for *Hamlet*, with Ralph saying 'We'll meet a couple of guards, and Hamlet's good friend Horatio. They are there because they want to see . . . .' But Sarah cuts off Ralph: 'let's not spoil it'. As a further guard against 'spoiling', the interviews usually keep characters separate from each other: Act 1 Scene 2 *myJulius Caesar* has three different interview groups, Caesar, Calpurnia and Antony; the Soothsayer; and Brutus and Cassius.

The hosts do not tell students or readers what to think: they allow each character to literally speak for him or herself. In each of the plays, the hosts are sometimes wry in their attitudes towards those they are interviewing, raising an ironic eyebrow, perhaps, but they are always prepared to listen straight-faced to whatever they are told. When *myJulius Caesar*'s Soothsayer is asked how he predicts the future using the liver of a ritually sacrificed animal, the Soothsayer replies, 'How else do you expect gods to communicate with us?' The interviewer moves on to the next question.

At other times, however, the Series Hosts are clearly concerned, even distressed, when they recognize inevitable outcomes in the [emerging] plot of the play. Because the interview is a re-running of the scene, bad things happen. 'Servilia' is Ralph's co-host for *myJulius Caesar*, and she is not happy telling Cinna the Poet what is happening to him in Act 3 Scene 3:

> SERVILIA: Oh, dear. Do we have to go through this again? 'Tear him. Tear him. Come; brands, ho! Firebrands. To Brutus', to Cassius', burn all. Decius' house, and some to some to Ligarius'. Away, go.' Okay. [Cinna the poet puts his head on the table, apparently dying, although the mob is not there] He's just a character,[28] right? Right?

The Series Hosts sometimes appear to have sympathies for one character more than others, as when Sarah looks disgusted with Capulet's clear satisfaction (Act 4 Scene 2) that Juliet has agreed to marry Paris. And Ralph seems a little desperate when he ends the *myMacbeth* Act 1 Scene 6 interview with Duncan and Lady Macbeth. The King has arrived at the castle oblivious that his murder is planned by the ambitious Macbeths. Ralph knows, and he opines that 'if I could just point out how lovely this arrival has been. It's really very sweet. And I hope everyone can see how good things can be, just the way they are. This, the status quo, is kind of awesome if you think about it'.

---

[28] What she means by character in this case is never explained.

These hosts suffer some personal peril as well. The weird sisters of *Macbeth* appear and disappear in lightning bolts, muttering charms and spooking Ralph. Ralph and Sarah make an early mistake in *myRomeo and Juliet* by having the Montagues and Capulets together in one room, an interview that ends in mayhem. At the conclusion of *myJulius Caesar*, Ralph decides it would be 'fun to check in one last time with the citizens of Rome' and discusses the conspiracy and resulting battles with them. The Plebeians realize that the interviewer knew about the assassination plot – and they are not happy (see Video 7). When Ralph can only claim he followed a 'non-interference policy', nervously repeating, 'I'm just the interviewer.' The same crowd that murdered Cinna the Poet now threatens Ralph, accusing him: 'You knew something was going on and you didn't do anything.' Ralph says to the camera, 'see you next time, if there is a next time', and makes a run offstage with the Plebeians in pursuit.

4.1.4 Text and Performance Combined

One teacher particularly commended the audio version in the edition for its clarity: the text is read slowly, with expression, but not with the fervour or pace of acted dialogue. This teacher reported that 'hearing the words read and using the glosses and other "hints" as needed, students

Video 7 The Plebeians will decide to attack Ralph, the series host, in *myShakespeare*. Video file is available at www.cambridge.org/turchi

realize that they don't have to understand every word to understand what is happening and why'. Watching the performance was not as important.

None of the teachers described asking their students to pay particular attention to what one called the 'real' performances embedded in the edition: the pop-up windows where students can see actors, in costumes, speaking to the camera and performing selected speeches and excerpts. Usually there is only the single actor, although there are some dialogues, and occasionally a third character may be in the screen. These performances seem largely directed at the reader, with the actors usually shot from the waist up, without props or scenery. The *myHamlet* production is the exception, with the performances on a stage and with characters focused on each other. One teacher referred to these performances as 'illustrations' of the play, a supplement to the audio provided for the full text.

The interviews were 'where my students really latched on', in the words of one teacher. Some teachers projected the interviews after the class had completed reading a scene, and several assigned students to watch the interviews as part of their homework. For these teachers there was a clear value to students in the ways that the interviews repeated and reinforced a scene. As one explained, 'You're giving kids the language that they don't quite understand [in the play], and then in the interview, they use the words and they make sense.'

Students also appreciated the body language in *myHamlet* interviews, for instance, where they could see a character's anger and frustration while also seeing the 'maintenance of civil discourse', as one teacher explained. Students like the interviews, according to one teacher, because 'You feel smart when you understand', and when the characters spoke with the Series Hosts the students heard the words – Shakespeare's language – and it made sense to them.

For students, the most significant performances in the *myShakespeare* interactive editions may be the interviews of the characters, in the studio and in 'on-the-scene' settings. A teacher who had previously assigned a scholarly critical edition of a play said that students often needed 'an explanation of those explanations' and in contrast they could watch the *myShakespeare* interviews and make sense for themselves.

4.1.5 Critical Thinking about Art and Intentionality

The Series Hosts consistently model critical thinking about the events of
the play and the characters' varying rationales for their actions. By their
very presence they remind students that *myShakespeare* is some kind of
production. On occasion, the Series Hosts also appeal to people behind the
camera, not exactly breaking a fourth wall but definitely indicating they
are not in the same world (space/time dimension?) as those being interviewed. There are unseen directors who are making production decisions
and are presumably in control, including deciding when they all can break
for lunch. They repeatedly refuse to let Ralph present a PowerPoint on
Shakespeare that he has apparently prepared. Only in rare moments do the
characters pay attention to the difference between themselves and the
hosts. In *myMidsummer Night's Dream* Puck uses an interview with
Athena the Host to try to pry out information about the whereabouts of
the lovers. Marullus, as a Tribune in *myJulius Caesar*, is very confident of
the dominance of Rome as an empire, and can't quite make sense of the
position of host:

MARULLUS:	This place you say you're from, is it a rich place?
SERVILIA:	Very.
MARULLUS:	And we've not conquered it yet?
SERVILIA:	Uh – no. That would be a little difficult to do.
[ALL LAUGH]	
MARULLUS:	I want you not to underestimate us. Could you show it to us on a map, perhaps?
SERVILIA:	I suppose.
MARULLUS:	Oh, my – that's pretty. What's that?
SERVILIA:	Oh, right. This is a phone. Uh –

The interview ends with the characters huddled over the cellphone,
entranced.

Teachers described modelling close reading with *myShakespeare* and
taking advantage of many of the supplementary links to point out that there
are multiple perspectives offered on the language as well as the plot. One

teacher assigned students to find 'remarkable language', and pointing to 'Word Nerd' videos as examples, such as the explanation of the phrase 'save your reverence' and the double *entendres* that alert readers to interestingly suggestive words.

In a classroom it might be useful to tell students that *myShakespeare* is an edition of Shakespeare *and* a cooperative film and editorial project. The glosses and modern, quite vernacular translations are collaboratively written by the team with help from 'smart undergraduates' (including some currently working on a Spanish-language modern translation for *myRomeo and Juliet*), according to Watkins, although this work is not explicitly credited to a team. Students might look at the cast biographies for each play, which indicate that the actors and crew are rising as well as established theatre and film professionals.

4.1.6 Social Learning through Theatre-Based Teaching Approaches

As much as teachers interviewed appreciated *myShakespeare* for what it offered students, they were clear about their continued loyalty to active approaches and their eagerness to return to 'on your feet' teaching of Shakespeare plays when the pandemic allowed. Several teachers described themselves as committed to activities they had learned through Folger Education in professional development venues. As one teacher noted, 'I learned Shakespeare through acting it out: get in there and read it. We have to *read* it together.' But teachers found ways that *myShakespeare* led to more independent reading, and more preparation for what one called 'asking and answering the big questions', however truncated online.

For instance, during hybrid instruction students had limited time to interact with the teacher and each other on a video platform.[29] In one virtual classroom students were urged to 'show emotion' when reading the text aloud, even while on Zoom, and the teacher felt *myShakespeare* provided particularly good models for how to read aloud. One teacher used *myShakespeare* with much-modified active approaches, such as starting

---

[29] Teachers reported using Zoom, Microsoft Teams and Google Meets as well as their districts' learning management systems.

a discussion of the opening of *Julius Caesar* with students choosing objects (from their homes, where they were) to represent different occupations. In this way they could feel added to the crowd celebrating Pompey; this teacher later used *myJulius Caesar* to highlight how the crowd of individuals becomes a mob.

4.1.7 Authentic Assessments of Student Learning

With reduced time 'in class' during the pandemic, teachers needed students to make the most of largely self-directed time, working individually answering character- and plot-based questions. Teachers told me that *myShakespeare* offered not only a way into a text through its combination of audio and video performances, but also opportunities for students to 'loop back' through the performances once they had gained familiarity with key words and ideas. *MyShakespeare* editions supported more than decoding: teachers described the platform as providing scaffolding for recursive reading, re-reading and otherwise engaging the play multiple times. As one teacher reported, 'I want my students to slow down and ask questions [of the text], and this edition encouraged them to do that.'

One teacher credited 'the innovative blending of Shakespeare's text and modern language' in the character interviews as 'fine examples for how students might demonstrate their knowledge of a given passage or scene'. Specifically, the *myShakespeare* notebook feature drew a lot of praise from teachers for supporting student writing, especially during pandemic teaching. Students could create a free account[30] that enabled additional icons. These opened to questions that checked for a reader's understanding of speeches and events. Multiple-choice questions also include the answers, with explanations for correct and incorrect selections. The questions require careful reading. The first question in *myMidsummer Night's Dream* Act 1 Scene 1 focuses on Theseus's complaint to Hippolyta about the delays to their marriage. The student can see all the choices and can open all the answers: the explanations for both correct and incorrect responses are helpful.

---

[30] Note that the site does publish a privacy policy: https://myshakespeare.com/privacy-policy

In *myMidsummer*, students are asked for a close reading of three lines. They are expected to note that in the text, 'young man's revenue' is glossed as 'inheritance', and so the incorrect answer here is not at all random.

> What is Theseus' complaint in lines 3–6?
>
> A. He has not yet received his inheritance.
> Incorrect
> Explanation: He is comparing the slowness with which the moon changes to the slowness of a young man gaining his inheritance from an aging, but slow-to-die stepmother or widow.
>
> B. Time is moving too slowly before his wedding to Hippolyta.
> Correct
> Explanation: In the first few lines, Theseus implies that he and Hippolyta will be married at the new moon. Then he complains 'how slow / This old moon wanes!' (lines 3–4). He wants the old moon to wane, or get smaller, faster so that the new moon will arrive and he can marry Hippolyta sooner.

In *myShakespeare* the student's work throughout the play can be recorded in the individual account notebook, and that includes a compilation of the questions and answers, with a link to each passage again in the context of the scene. There are no scores or grades – just an indication whether the student has completed the question by selecting the correct answer. Teachers reported that students liked how these questions assured them that 'they got it' when it came to understanding the play. One teacher reported university students also thought that the questions, even when used 'just' to check understanding, required slower and more thoughtful reading than expected.

There are also open-ended questions labelled as a 'written quiz' that highlight character development or ask students about events and consequences. Teachers can assign these and then collect the responses through the notebook functions: students may export a PDF of their answers and submit these to a classroom's learning management system.

myHamlet 4.4 asks about Fortinbras, for instance:

> Given what has happened so far, what purpose do you think
> Fortinibras serves in the play? Defend your answer with
> textual evidence.

In addition to capturing student writing, the notebook feature enables
students to create tags or labels for different scenes or selections from
speeches. Students can search for their tags in the play and create PDFs
of their notebooks as evidence of their work. They can collect their
responses to different prompts, and other notes, and use colour-coding to
organize these, perhaps into potential evidence for important themes.
Students can also cut and paste sections from the text into the notebook,
so that they can buttress their reasoning and arguments with direct quotations from the text.

Teachers reported that they assigned notebook-based activities to
support students' preparation for writing tasks that require them to
synthesize their learning. One teacher described a recurring virtual
instructional cycle, where students read some of the play aloud, were
required to annotate scenes, watched film clips outside of the edition,
and completed *myShakespeare* writing assignments every week.
Students' not having to re-type quotes was described as 'a big plus'.
Because of distance learning, this teacher was not able to monitor
student progress as closely as usual, so some students may not have
kept up with the note-taking all along in the *myShakespeare* notebook.
However students discovered that writing the final essay assignment
was much easier if they had.

Teachers saw evidence of student learning from *myShakespeare* in
formative and summative assessments, especially where the prompt
demanded textual evidence. These teachers were pleased that
myShakespeare supported 'genuine extended discussions' in their virtual
classrooms, with students who remembered specific scenes and even
speeches more easily. Students who could only communicate with each
other (and the teacher) via asynchronous discussion boards and other

online tools demonstrated their interest in topics from revenge to regime change while integrating references to their Shakespeare readings.

Several teachers said that teaching in the pandemic meant they could not assign a 'big' assignment to mark the end of a Shakespeare unit – neither a major paper, nor an extended creative project, as would be usual in their classroom. For teachers who assign students to research and present perspectives from secondary sources of literary criticism, the *myHamlet* is the only play in the edition to include scholarly perspectives. There are citations of critical perspectives from Harold Bloom and Marjorie Garber in one video titled 'Why It's Cool' – Meditation on Two Themes (3.1) To Be or Not to Be'. In this video an animated Ralph and Sarah discuss Hamlet's apparent consideration of suicide, his desire for revenge, and his speculations on the larger human condition (see Video 8). Ralph suggests that Hamlet is 'always connecting his specific life to questions about life in general', which is an idea that many student writers are assigned to explore.

One teacher chose not to assign or discuss any of the supporting videos or other materials beyond the immediate text of the play and annotations made

Video 8 In *myHamlet* the animated hosts discuss Hamlet's suicidal tendencies. Video file is available at www.cambridge.org/turchi

using the notebook feature. This teacher did not know how many students listened to the audio or watched the performances. It was not that students couldn't use the other features, but the teacher did not encourage them to explore these options. This is an important reminder of the navigational realities of all digital editions of Shakespeare: no one necessarily needs to use any specific feature, nor access these in a specified order, to meet instructional goals. While ambitious teaching would encourage students to make use of all the available resources, students could also be tasked with exploration, and to make meaning in ways that made sense to them.

4.2 Whole Selves of Students

4.2.1 Access to Shakespeare

One teacher described struggling to teach *Romeo and Juliet* to ninth graders (13–14 year-olds) who were reading at the 4th–5th grade level. Teaching in a low-wealth public high school, with real limits to available technology in the school, this teacher could have no expectation that students would have access to a laptop or desktop at home. However, this teacher found students did have access to good phones, and luckily their individual devices worked well with *myShakespeare*. This teacher discovered that students even recommended *myShakespeare* to friends in other classes studying the play using only a textbook.

There are some teachers who find Shakespeare plays onerous or intimidating, often because their own early experiences with The Bard included endless lectures or difficult independent passage work. Using *myShakespeare* offers teachers a chance to escape those unsuccessful years. As one teacher told me, 'The play's the thing indeed!' referring to *myShakespeare* admiringly as not being 'Laurence Olivier Shakespeare'. Teachers appreciated how the edition depicted what one called 'true playing', particularly given the stresses of the pandemic in their virtual classrooms.

One teacher using *myShakespeare* described the pleasure of working with an ESL (English as a Second Language) paraprofessional. In that class, the emergent bilingual students seemed to especially like to work with the edition. The paraprofessional would help translate what the characters were saying, especially in the interviews. This work culminated in the students creating their own interview: an entirely Spanish interview between Tybalt, Romeo and Mercutio.

Teachers also described their students as appreciating 'the humour and hipness'. As one teacher said, 'All of us attempt to make Shakespeare approachable, and as English nerds, we want to ask, "How do you NOT like Shakespeare?"' This edition made it possible for students to feel that the jokes were as much for them as for an expert reader. 'If you "get" what's going on, the parody advertisements are funny commentary on and amplification of the situation that's being depicted in the play', according to one teacher. Another recommended showing the *Hamlet* commercial for Imperial Match.com, especially with its slogan: 'we'll find your soulmate, and still make it look arranged'. Teachers found their students highly responsive to Shakespeare plays taught using *myShakespeare* because these were not 'too leatherbound' as editions: everyone could be in on the jokes and conceits and entertaining side comments that are embedded throughout the edition.

4.2.2 Identity and Cultural Relevance

The *myShakespeare* editions also use short, animated films to suggest connections between students and the play. For instance, they encourage students to imagine themselves in Shakespeare's original audience. In *myJulius Caesar* the feature on 'Clothing Laws' describes the relationships among work and dress and status, and it explains how in Shakespeare's day (like in the Rome of the play) work and home are the same place. The short film that is tied to *Macbeth* Act 4 Scene 3, references 'strangely visited people' and the belief that a King can cure disease through 'touching'. Ambitious teaching might suggest that this is relevant for discussing the proliferation of Covid cures and other online medical advice. One teacher found that students were impressed with the background about the finances of acting companies like Shakespeare's in the video on Elizabethan theatre and wanted to discuss popular art and different markers of success.

The casting of the actors in *myShakespeare* helps twenty-first-century students further identify with the works. 'The kids saw themselves', according to one teacher, and understood 'that different kinds of people could play the different characters'. As another opportunity for ambitious teaching, it's worth noting that the casting can enable teachers to talk about colour- and gender-blind casting in a way very specific to *myShakespeare*: the interviews cannot interrogate casting at all. The point is that it's the character being interviewed, not the actor. When Brutus is Black and female, but the play text is not altered, students can consider whether and how that matters to their interpretations. *Julius Caesar* is not often discussed as a 'race play', and yet the animated 'Who's Who in Rome' may help students think about representation and power as they compare the setting of the play to London, where it was first performed, and to their own schools and homes (see Video 9). Discussions might also draw out what students notice about the accents of the players, and the impact their performances have on the imaginations of readers, who may expect 'Shakespeare' to sound quite different.

While the isolation of pandemic learning often meant that reading literature felt both 'hard' and 'long' with less of the dynamism of classroom

Video 9 The Montagues and Capulets together for an interview (that ends disastrously) in *myShakespeare*. Note the diversity of the casting. Video file is available at www.cambridge.org/turchi

conversation and activities, teachers felt that students were still able to gain understanding and appreciation through *myShakespeare*. The *myShakespeare* interactive editions might appear to be 'self-teaching', given the wealth of resources available for every speech and scene, but the teachers interviewed discussed using the editions in face-to-face as well as online classes, supporting students towards different levels of independence. Teachers interviewed for this section were quite sure that using *myShakespeare* editions had enabled their students to feel they understood the work more readily. The students also told teachers that they found it more enjoyable than they had expected.

Although the necessity of virtual classrooms during the pandemic challenged many teachers, the *myShakespeare* editions clearly gave students additional tools for making meaning. One teacher said that at the conclusion of one Shakespeare unit 'we talked for a whole hour in both classes', no small accomplishment in an online literature class. Teachers described students 'taking ownership' and showing a real familiarity and confidence with dense scenes that seemed very remote from their lives. As one teacher said, after using *myShakespeare* students now 'did seem to believe there was a lot to this play'.

Multiple teachers described new thinking about their instructional strategies arising from using *myShakespeare*. They planned, back in face-to-face classrooms, to highlight 'bigger questions' in the plays beyond plot and character identification. Teachers felt they could hone-in on what students needed and wanted to think about and remember. Looking ahead to classroom life after the pandemic, teachers also described drawing on *myShakespeare* to support student-favourite projects like creating alternative stagings and endings for *Romeo and Juliet* or collaboratively filming *Julius Caesar* as a comedy. This kind of re-storying Shakespeare, where students are encouraged to rethink and reset Shakespeare plays to their own contexts, is supported by the *myShakespeare* curriculum guides, also embedded in the editions in a section labelled 'For Teachers'. The curriculum guides include passages for discussing the staging of key scenes (with links back to *myShakespeare* editions), and Act-by-Act discussion questions and writing prompts for moving students into more complex analysis comparing characters and articulating their motivations. But there are also many suggestions for creative student work, such as through incorporating Snapchat or podcasting to create their own interviews in 'You Be the Host'. As it was for the emergent bilingual students described in this section, there may be no better way for students to talk with, and back to, Shakespeare plays than through creating their own dialogues and scenes, incorporating the work into their own understanding and lives.

5 Three Case Studies for Ambitious Teaching

5.1 Useful Teaching Tools

The three case studies in this Element contrast interactive digital editions of Shakespeare, and each describes how teachers reported integrating an edition into online and in-person classroom practices. The cases provide evidence that all three editions offer students authentic academic engagement. The editions present both the text and a performance of a Shakespeare play and provide supplemental synopses, glosses, translations, and more that encourage independent meaning-making. Further, the editions are each a site for critical thinking: about edition-creating, and theatre-making, and the arts of performance. The productions embedded in each edition are cast with diverse actors, providing a starting place for students to discuss identity and the claims about Shakespeare as universal. By providing so many aids for understanding a Shakespeare text and performance, each edition makes Shakespeare plays more accessible for more learners. All these characteristics potentially support ambitious teaching. That is, the editions can be assets in twenty-first-century classrooms that are concerned with rigorous close readings and the kinds of discussions and activities that contemporary students want to engage in.

Although the editions share many characteristics, teachers describe them differently when recounting their use in their classrooms. *WordPlay Shakespeare*, with its book-like interactive design, helped teachers who sought to increase independent student comprehension of the play text. *PerformancePlus*, which combines a recorded theatrical performance with the play text, helped focus student attention on characterization, on the ways that a text is brought to life through skilful acting. Finally, *myShakespeare*, an edition that provides extensive glosses and supplemental information combined with an audio performance, as well as a video recap of each scene by way of interviews with characters, was especially useful to teachers seeking to prepare students for more sophisticated dialogue and writing. The edition enabled students to pay attention to themes and motivations rather than plots and simple character identification.

Other commonalities in the use of the editions further indicate how interactive editions can support ambitious teaching. Teachers described integrating the interactive edition into sophisticated instruction that also included complementary readings or other digital tools. One used the *EduPuzzle* programme to create segments of recorded performances from Shakespeare's Globe to supplement the edition. Another teacher compiled three different filmed versions of the assassination of Julius Caesar to highlight directing choices. In one classroom, the interactive edition helped students make connections between the play and Chinua Achebe's *Things Fall Apart* and Albert Camus's *The Stranger*, read earlier in the semester. Teachers appreciated having 'all the support in one place' from glosses and hyperlinks, even as they described supplementing the edition with their own materials: 'I can drop in *my* things,' one teacher noted, because the digital edition was a tool, not a curriculum.

When one school's online schedule greatly reduced synchronous time, a teacher assigned students to read *Hamlet* using *MyShakespeare* for Act 1 and *PerformancePlus* for Act 2. The students wrote briefly about their preferences and what they would choose for continuing in the play. They repeatedly referenced their appreciation for the translated words, the immediately available synonyms and definitions that allowed them to move through the scenes with more ease. The students compared the audio to video formats, and they liked that they could choose which suited them. They said they used the formats differently as they progressed through scenes: some started with audio as they read, then for another scene watched the performance first, in order to 'see the emotions'. Some used the study questions to get ideas for writing, while others used the character interviews to be sure they understood what a particular character seemed to want. One student described using the platforms 'in unison' – opening one on a computer, and the other on a phone, using one edition for the performance and the other for the text with all its glosses.

Describing their online teaching during the pandemic, teachers said they were limited: they struggled to ignite dynamic discussions, coach extended writing tasks, and lead theatre-based activities. But most credited the interactive editions for providing a foundation, a starting place, for what kinds of ambitious practices they were able to maintain. The teachers described the editions as helping their students successfully understand and even enjoy Shakespeare's complicated texts. Teachers from smaller, more geographically remote places also appreciated the interactive editions because their communities did not have access to Shakespeare performances, with or without a pandemic.

Yet it is important to recognize how much the pandemic cost Shakespeare instruction in secondary schools, thwarting the intentions of expert, enthusiastic teachers. As described by one teacher, teaching *Romeo and Juliet* to students as their first Shakespeare requires using a combination of presentation, dialogue, classroom acting (with a great collection of props), student reflections and study guides, and innovative, creative final projects. Unable to meet directly with students to engage them in these usual ways, this teacher felt the interactive editions made students too passive. While other teachers were far more enthusiastic about what the editions offered, they too felt that strictly independent use of an interactive edition would be a poor substitute for real in-person teaching.

5.2 Interactive Editions and Instructional Designs

As much as the editions offer, they are not comprehensive. Brett Hirsch and colleagues (2017) suggest we consider all that a digital edition of a Shakespeare play might potentially include:

> Imagine that the script/play-text of each of these videos has been transcribed and is fully searchable, such that a user is able to quickly navigate between instances of the word across the entire corpus, and thereby able to quickly compare different film and stage interpretations. Imagine the inclusion of

additional layers of metadata – bibliographical information, as well as details and observations on technical aspects of the performances, such as lighting; music and sound; set design and location; costuming; camera angle; special effects; etc – all tied to the videos in time-specific, fully searchable utterances. Imagine the ability to add and search through user-generated annotations, commentary, tags, and ratings, or to create and share bookmarks and incorporate them in student assignments and scholarly articles. Imagine linking primary, secondary, and ancillary materials to the video(s) and text(s), again in time-specific, fully searchable utterances. Imagine the integration of film and theatre reviews, transcribed and fully searchable, keyed to the play(s) and performance(s) discussed – users given the opportunity to critically assess and compare review(s), available as subjects for study in and of themselves. Such an electronic scholarly edition would offer an invaluable resource for students and scholars of Shakespearean film and television, performance studies and criticism, adaptation studies, and theatre history. (p. 7)

Would such an all-encompassing edition be useful to ambitious classroom teaching? Of course. But these cases suggest that such a trove of resources would still not replace a teacher, especially for students who are new to Shakespeare plays. The editions in these cases do save teachers from an 'explainer' role – one which we know diminishes student engagement and independent meaning-making. Ambitious teaching means designing activities and discussions so that the rich but complicated syntax and vocabulary on the page becomes more manageable; the characters emerge as multidimensional human beings; the plotlines illustrate understandable, if not rational, choices; and there are themes – not universal so much as recognizable perspectives on human experience – that the reader can embrace or critique. Interactive editions can help meet these goals.

There are models for classrooms, such as a 'flipped' instructional design, that suggest possibilities for post-pandemic teaching with, rather than replaced by, interactive editions. Classroom instruction is said to be flipped when students are expected to watch online lectures or other videos outside of class. This viewing is intended to be preparation for interactive, discussion-filled class time, where the focus can be on their engagement in group and other dynamic activities (see Shaffer 2016, for further description and discussion). Several teachers interviewed for this Element had experimented with a flipped design using interactive Shakespeare editions before the pandemic closed their classrooms and made independent reading more of a necessity. In one design, students used an interactive edition to read a section of a Shakespeare play on their own, and sometimes they would be required to show proof of their work before class started. The teacher would then lead class discussion based on the common knowledge of a specific text: as a result, class time happily, to this teacher, meant 'spending more time on constructive conversation'. In another version of flipping, students had time during class to read the play using the interactive edition, and the teacher designated specific stopping points that students reached, wrote about, and then discussed. These designs also included time for theatre-based exercises.

5.3 Interactive Editions and Future Teachers

These teaching models are like those my own students, future English teachers, envisioned after their experiences with the three interactive editions. For several semesters, before and during the pandemic, these students explored the editions both to refresh their knowledge of *Romeo and Juliet* and to think about the possible advantages of using interactive editions in their classrooms. The pre-service teachers have consistently told me they wished the interactive editions had been available to them as high school students, that these would have reduced their 'struggle and frustration' with Shakespeare. They remembered Shakespeare plays read aloud for what felt like hours and hours in their own high school classes. As one noted compassionately, 'it was hard to listen to classmates and myself struggle with rhythm and pronunciation. But, it did teach patience, understanding, and empathy. I would catch myself rooting for other classmates to do well'.

Future teachers also recounted being silent in class discussions, too unsure of what the words meant to speak up. They described listening to a teacher's explanation and then struggling to find and write about 'the right lines' because they did not see a connection between what they were told and what they were trying to read. These students offered insights into why the pairing of the text and performance seemed valuable. One described hearing more than just sadness, for instance, in a performance. By watching Juliet as well as reading her lines, the reader/viewer discovered the character was not only sad, but angry, was blaming herself for falling in love with the 'wrong' person. As a result, wrote the student teacher, much more of the words in the speech made sense. Another wrote,

> I found these resources absolutely groundbreaking. It changes everything to have access to a tool that does not just cater to one learning type but offers audio and visual options as well as countless other resources to aid understanding. . . . I can imagine that students probably respect us a little more when we give them extra tools and communicate that we understand their struggles and find them valid.

Few of my students advocated for just watching a movie or performance. One wrote it was disappointing when a teacher showed a film instead of asking them to read the 'actual Shakespeare play'. I promote ambitious teaching with these teachers-in-training, reminding them that the goal is to foster *student* facilities with Shakespeare, and that this requires deliberately weaning everyone from a 'teacher as expert' mentality. The scaffolding for independent reading that an interactive digital edition provides is neither 'cheating' nor stealing from a teacher's rightful role. Using the editions does require opportunities for students to explore the tools that are available and determine what information is useful for each individual reader.

5.4 Independent Meaning-Making

With the interactivity of a digital edition, the flow of learning is not restricted to teachers informing students. Writing this Element provided a luxury of time to try out and describe what each includes. While the catalogue of features here is reasonably complete, the editions are regularly updated with new features. The richness of digital edition resources means that it is necessary and good that students explore and discover on their own what is available and what is helpful to them. Ambitious teaching would not require staying 'ahead' of students, guiding them explicitly to every sidebar or gloss.

Students need to follow their own paths of learning. Future teachers, as well as students in a college course experimenting with *myShakespeare*, appreciated the interactive editions because they were 'efficient'. One described being a reader/viewer who could 'easily see what each of the unfamiliar words meant in relation to the rest of the sentence and play'. Students describe a wealth of personal navigational choices. Some wrote that they would read scene summaries first, while some watched the performance first. Some kept a modern translation open at the same time they viewed the production. And many reported increased confidence as they worked through a play:

> 'I got used to the language and learned what it meant. Now, I do not look at the modern English version, I am just able to read along.' 'Now since I know most of the language/slang that they use, I don't have to read the summaries which makes it faster for me to comprehend and move on.' 'Before I would read the actual play, then watch the clip and read the summary. But now, I watch the clip and read the actual play at the same time, then after that I read through the modern English and page summary. Lastly, I do the questions at the end.'

Teachers described other affordances in using the interactive digital editions with their classes. With the editions, high school students who had been absent from class (in pre-Covid days, especially) were not at a disadvantage. Teachers found it remarkable that students would now 'actually keep up with the play' if they were absent. Gone were jarring holes in student plot summaries or character descriptions because of missed class discussions. One teacher shared the link to *PerformancePlus* as a way for students to catch up, telling them, 'You'll miss the analysis and interaction, but at least you won't be completely in the dark.' Teachers noted that before the pandemic students would resist reading the play on their own. The editions enabled students to work at their own pace.

Some educators wished that the edition included more interaction built into the platform: that what some might assume is the teacher's responsibility should be imitated by more interactive requirements on the part of the reader. For instance, students might be stopped from moving forward in a text until they answered questions or responded to other prompts. Some teachers have qualms about too much student independence. They worry it is a disservice to students to 'just send them off' with the edition, with no guidance or feedback on what they are understanding. To counteract this, one teacher interviewed described working closely with the students and the interactive edition for the first acts – asking students about the meaning of specific symbolism, about whether they understood connections between events, and asking for predictions, for instance. By the third act, the teacher described 'backing off' and asking more open-ended questions that required students to cite particular lines.

Teachers recognized that interactive editions helped students be more confident about not only about what was happening in a play, but why; more sure of what characters meant when they spoke, and able to catch nuance in metaphoric language and literary allusions. In this way, it seems clear that interactive editions enable ambitious teaching to expand and complicate how we understand Shakespeare plays, rather than reducing and simplifying, for instance by way of a modern translation.

5.5 Interactive Editions and Student Writing

Academic engagement does not have to only happen in discussion. Teachers described the written work that they assigned students to accompany reading a Shakespeare play, and the assessments they made of student learning. Given their emergency online teaching situations, some of the teachers I interviewed said they omitted their usual quizzes on character and quote identification. But most teachers interviewed still expected students to engage with the text through note-taking and other short arguments of literary interpretation described under an umbrella term of *annotating*. Sometimes these notes are an end product in themselves; other times the annotations are steppingstones to more extensive writing. While the assignment of annotating varies among teachers, the common dimensions were asking students to note key passages, to recognize and highlight literary devices and other important language (such as revealing 'writer's craft'), and to write briefly about a passage's connection to a theme. The interactive editions made spaces for considerations of theatre-making, instances where students would think critically about decisions and designs for presenting a Shakespeare play. Assignments gave students reasons to review both text and performance. And while an annotating process is typically a writing-to-learn strategy for students, these assignments contributed to writing about the text more comprehensively, or better yet, adapting or re-storying the work, as described below.

Ambitious teaching of a Shakespeare play would encourage students to notice disagreements, even scholarly uncertainty, about how to interpret a line or speech. Interactive editions support this kind of openness to interpretation by helping a reader make sense rather than insisting on what a passage means. Teachers described how students used interactive editions to look for cues that matched the text to the acting, learning to pry apart the text from the performance. There are also digital tools that students can use to catalogue and prepare to debate their insights. There are the 'notebook' features built into *WordPlay Shakespeare* and *myShakespeare*, and teachers described using Google Docs to capture student notes and commentary as well.

Given the accessibility of such tools, students can collaborate as editors, creating their own editions. In many ways, they already do so. Everyone who has filled a printed text with marginalia and made a personal index of important pages, as well as students filling notebooks or study guides, are all creating editions – personal interfaces to capture careful reading. In this sense, creating an edition is not about authoritative scholarship but is more like leaving breadcrumbs – as a guide, but also evidence – of what mattered about a text at the time. Students can puzzle over how to choose the right information to include in order to be useful, which opens discussions about what makes an edition authoritative. Ann Christensen and I argue that it is appropriate and useful to engage students in dialogues about what an edition reveals and perhaps conceals, particularly when it uses language that is objectionable to twenty-first-century ears (f2023, p. 506). As teachers we can proactively locate the places in a text with racist language and use editing discussions to prepare ourselves to address what we might otherwise want to apologize for or avoid. Similarly, Patricia Akhimie writes of her students creating editions of Shakespeare plays and practicing 'thinking of yourself as an expert' (2021, p.n/a). Akhimie finds that students of colour especially need to see their experiences and perspectives represented in a text.

5.6 Talking Back to Shakespeare

As has probably become obvious, this Element does not seek one interactive edition to rule all, but is rather ambitious for teachers to advocate for further digital integration and meaningful multimodal work in their schools. In an earlier case study, I described watching students use *WordPlay Shakespeare* as the basis of creative student work. The students used iMovie (available on the class iPads) to create trailers for imagined films that focused on one character. The assignment resulted in a wide variety of responses: there was a stop-action chase through a Lego-built forest, Egeus illustrated by clips from Presidential campaign news stories, favourite teachers cast as Hermia and Lysander, Oberon portrayed in a prismatic selection of Google images, and mash-ups that included *WordPlay* screenshots.

Re-storying is not a radical idea for English Language Arts classrooms, as student-created 'modern re-tellings' of Shakespeare have a long tradition. I should probably confess that the most vivid Shakespeare learning I did in high school was in a skit, where our group repurposed *Julius Caesar* Act 3 Scene 1– the assassination – to explain the origins of the Caesar salad. As we were all Monty Python fans, I'm sure our humour was sick and our faithfulness to the text questionable. When I talk to adults about what they remember from Shakespeare in school, it's enacting scenes and adapting texts to current contexts, creating art and multimodal projects that were as much a commentary on their own lives as performances of a canonical work.

Interactive editions can make room for re-storying in a Shakespeare unit. Students can discuss and reflect on the ways that the new works are 'true' as both adaptions of the original text and as expressions of what life is like in these times. Ambitious teaching can create assignments where students' lived perspectives matter. Shakespeare plays in adaptation can be counterstories: Jean Dyches Bissonnette and Jocelyn Glazier want teachers to encourage students to counterstory dominant narratives, asserting their own perspectives and experiences as worthy for consideration and as useful stances for critiques (2016, p. 686). As Jean Dyches describes, when classrooms celebrate a traditional, canonical author like Shakespeare, remaking a play (or scene or speech) into new versions can ensure that there are also spaces where social consciousness is raised, and students do not need to feel erased (2017, p. 300). Ebony Elizabeth Thomas and Amy Stornaiuolo write, 'As scholars working from postmodern, critical, feminist, and critical race perspectives, we note that women, people of color, and other marginalized readers have always had to read themselves into canons that excluded them' (2016, p. 317). Interactive editions have the potential to support far more inclusive readings. Wayne Slabon and colleagues emphasize iterative processes of restorying in the classroom, highlighting ways that the combination of personal and 'official' stories, written and discussed, can spur critical thinking and creative problem solving (2014, p. 506).

Interactive digital editions emphasize that there are many stories, many interpretations, and with them students can escape the idea, as expressed by Chimamanda Ngozi Adichie, that there is only one story to be told, one universal expression that would 'speak' for generalized human experience (2009). Teachers should not be burdened with defending The Bard as a definitive and singular literary deity: Shakespeare does not hold beneficial truth for everyone. As Kim Hall and Peter Erickson remind us, 'Even if the arc of our moral universe bends toward justice, it may be that Shakespeare's moral universe does not bend far enough to go the distance needed now' (2016, p. 10).

Interactive editions of Shakespeare support ambitious teaching: they provide tools for the methods and strategies that, combined with high expectations, bring more students to success. As a teacher educator, it is painful to recognize how the early frustrations of student teaching, especially when fledgling teachers feel tested by classroom management, sometimes plant the seeds of low expectations. I want student teachers to be surprised by how interactive digital editions provide methods for grabbing the interest and focusing the attention of students at all reading levels. Mentors of student teachers, and their education professors, need to do more to disrupt assumptions that a student's performance is bounded by class, race, or other descriptors. Some future teachers give me hope by expressing their strong commitments to equity. One student teacher described growing up in a low-income community, and wrote, 'Our parents did not have the time, money or even the knowledge to take us to a professional theater production. ... My favorite thing about these platforms is that they expose students to something they may not have access to otherwise.'

5.7 *Where Further Research Is Needed*

As one student wrote to me, 'In all honesty, I am still working on my relationship with Shakespearean plays.' There are, of course, teachers who have access to interactive editions of Shakespeare and choose not to use them. Or they may try them once with students, but not continue. As I described from earlier case study work, I visited a district and spoke with teachers about a wide range of strategies for implementation. But there were – are – always teachers who choose not to appear at such invitational meetings and who, their colleagues report, decide not to use the edition at all. It is difficult to know why, but it is easy to imagine frustration or bafflement in general with technology, dismay that students are difficult to corral and keep safe when they are online, worries about looking foolish when students navigate more intuitively than we do, and other variations on the fear of losing control. And there's Shakespeare, of course: too hard for students? Too much to cover? Too little relevance?

I have made multiple efforts to partner with local school systems to more formally gauge the impact of interactive digital editions on teachers and perhaps on students. Small scale, comfortably voluntary initiatives are generally welcome, but broader more scientific scrutiny has been thwarted consistently at district levels. There are many competing priorities, and many ways that administrators are too stretched to care much about the specific curriculum and texts. What's more, it's clear that students (and teachers) can use these interactive editions in widely varying, personally useful ways. The kinds of standardization that an empirical study would require may not be worth it. But I believe these are lost opportunities, because new or improved success with Shakespeare plays likely has a measurable impact on students and teachers. Interactive editions could increase teacher expectations for what their students can do and accomplish; students can gain stronger belief in their own agency. It may even be possible to map Shakespeare success onto standardized test scores, connecting the plays to what school culture is forced to value (whether it should or not is another question).

My own work now includes helping develop other digital tools, working with theatre companies who, especially during the pandemic, have been forced to put more of their offerings online, create more virtual classroom supports in their education outreach. The teachers who have made this Element possible have given me endless ideas and powerful insights into what their students need and how their classrooms might utilize interactive editions in engaging ways. In the end, what I believe teachers want are pathways to great Shakespeare discussions: ones that are rich with the text, with performances, and with connections students make to our lives today.

References

Adichie, C. N. (2009). *The Danger of a Single Story*. TEDGlobal. https://
www.ted.com/talks/chimamanda_ngozi_adichie_the_danger_of_a_sin
gle_story?utm_campaign=tedspread&utm_medium=referral&utm_
source=tedcomshare.

Akhimie, P. (2021). 'Cultivating Expertise: Glossing Shakespeare and
Race'. *Literature Compass Special Issue*, 18(10), https://doi.org/10.1111
/lic3.12607.

Bissonnette, J. D., and J. Glazier (2016). 'A Counterstory of One's Own'.
Journal of Adolescent & Adult Literacy, [Online] 59(6), 685–94.

Christensen, A., and L. B. Turchi (2023). 'Re-editing the Renaissance for an
Anti-racist Classroom'. In A. Wainwright and M. Chapman (eds.). *Race
in the European Renaissance: A Classroom Guide*. Tempe AZ Arizona
Center for Medieval and Renaissance Studies: ACMRS Press, 505-24.

Dakin, M. E. (2012). *Reading Shakespeare Film First*. Urbana, IL: National
Council of Teachers of English.

Dyches, J. (2017). 'Shaking Off Shakespeare: A White Teacher, Urban
Students, and the Mediating Powers of a Canonical
Counter-Curriculum'. *The Urban Review*, [Online] 49(2), 300–25.

Erickson, P. and K. F. Hall (2016). '"A New Scholarly Song": Rereading
Early Modern Race'. *Shakespeare Quarterly*, 67(1), 1–13.

Estill, L. (2019). 'Digital Resource Reviews / Comptes Rendus Sur Les
Ressources Numeriques Introduction: Special Issue, Digital Shakespeare
Texts'. *Renaissance and Reformation*, 42(3), 167–74.

Gee, J. P. (2017). 'Affinity Spaces and 21st-Century Learning.' *Educational
Technology*, 57 (2), 27–31. www.jstor.org/stable/44430520.

Hirsch, B., S. Arneil, and G. Newton. (2017). '"Mark the Play": Electronic Editions of Shakespeare and Video Content'. *Scholarly and Research Communication*, 8(2). https://doi.org/10.22230/src.2017v8n2a279.

Hope, J. (2003). *Shakespeare's Grammar*. London: Bloomsbury Arden Shakespeare.

Kennedy, M. M., T. D. Pigott, and A. M. Ryan. (2019). 'How We Learn About Teacher Learning'. *Review of Research in Education*, 43(1), 138–62.

Kidnie, M. J. (2018). 'The Stratford Festival of Canada: Mental Tricks and Archival Documents in the Age of NTLive'. In P. Aebischer, S. Greenhaigh, and L. E. Osborne (eds.). *Shakespeare and the 'Live' Theatre Broadcast Experience*. London: Bloomsbury Arden Shakespeare, 133–46.

Lampert, M., and F. Graziani. (2009). 'Instructional Activities as a Tool for Teachers' and Teacher Educators' Learning'. *The Elementary School Journal*, 109(5), 491–509.

Lampert, M., M. L. Franke, E. Kazemi, et al. (2013). 'Keeping It Complex: Using Rehearsals to Support Novice Teacher Learning of Ambitious Teaching'. *Journal of Teacher Education*, 64(3), 226–243, https://doi.org/10.1177/0022487112473837.

Lior, N. (2019). *Mediating for Immediacy: Text, Performance, and Dramaturgy in Multimedia Shakespeare Editions*. ProQuest Dissertations. www.proquest.com/dissertations-theses/mediating-immediacy-text-performance-dramaturgy/docview/2316417379/se-2.

Lior, N. (2020). 'Multimedia Shakespeare Editions: Making Shakespeare Accessible/Making an Accessible Shakespeare'. *Research in Drama Education*, 25(1), 125–42.

Loewenberg Ball, D., and F. M. Forzani (2009). 'The Work of Teaching and the Challenge for Teacher Education'. *Journal of Teacher Education*, 60(5), 497–511. https://doi.org/10.1177/0022487109348479.

Long, K., and M. T. Christel (2019). *Bring on the Bard: Active Drama Approaches for Shakespeare's Diverse Student Readers*. Urbana, IL: National Council of Teachers of English.

Marcus, L. S. (1996). *Unediting the Renaissance: Shakespeare, Marlowe, Milton*. London: Routledge.

Massai, S. (2017). 'Editing Shakespeare in Parts'. *Shakespeare Quarterly*. 68 (1), 56–79.

Neville, S. (2018). 'Rethinking Scholarly Commentary in the Age of Google: Some Preliminary Meditations on Digital Editions'. *Textual Cultures: Text, Contexts, Interpretation*, 12(1), 1–26.

Orgel, S. (2007). 'The Desire and Pursuit of the Whole'. *Shakespeare Quarterly*, 58(3), 290–310.

Paris, D. (2016). 'Culturally Sustaining Pedagogy: A Needed Change in Stance, Terminology, and Practice'. *Educational Researcher*, 41(3), 93–97.

Richmond, G., T. Bartell, R. Floden, and E. Petchauer. (2017). 'Core Teaching Practices: Addressing Both Social Justice and Academic Subject Matter'. *Journal of Teacher Education*, 68(5), 432–34, https://doi .org/10.1177/0022487117732950.

Romeo and Juliet, dir F. Zeffirelli, Paramount Pictures 1968.

Royster, F. T. (2011). 'Comic Terror and Masculine Vulnerability in "Slings and Arrows: Season Three"'. *Journal of Narrative Theory*, 41(3), 343–61. https://doi.org/10.1353/jnt.2011.0100.

Schneier, L. (2021). 'Give Them the Butterflies'. In M. K. Delaney and S. J. Mayer (eds.). *In Search of Wonderful Ideas: Critical Explorations in Teacher Education*. New York: Teachers College Press, 74–84.

Shaffer, S. (2016). 'One High School English Teacher: On His Way to a Flipped Classroom'. *Journal of Adolescent & Adult Literacy*, 59(5), 563–73.

Shepard, L. A. (2021). 'Ambitious Teaching and Equitable Assessment: A Vision for Prioritizing Learning, Not Testing'. *American Educator*, 45 (3), 28–32.

Simonetta, R. D., and M. Lo. (2022). 'The Shakespeare CoLab: A Digital Learning Environment for Shakespeare Studies'. In D. E. Henderson and K. S. Vitale (eds.). *Shakespeare and Digital Pedagogy: Case Studies and Strategies*. London: Bloomsbury Arden Shakespeare, 25–37.

Slabon, W., R. Richards and V. Dennen (2014). 'Learning by Restorying'. *Instructional Science*, 42(4), 505–521. https://doi-org.ezproxy.lib.uh.edu /10.1007/s11251-014-9311-z.

Thomas, E. E., and A. Stornaiuolo. (2016). 'Restorying the Self: Bending Toward Textual Justice'. *Harvard Educational Review* 86(3), 313–38.

Thompson, A., and L. Turchi. (2016). *Teaching Shakespeare with Purpose: A Student-Centred Approach*. London: Bloomsbury Arden Shakespeare.

Thompson, J., M. Windschitl, and M. Braaten. (2013). 'Developing a Theory of Ambitious Early-Career Teacher Practice'. *American Educational Research Journal*, 50(3), 574–615, https://doi.org/10.3102 /0002831213476334.

Turchi, L. B. (2020). 'Shakespeare e-Books Engage Students and Support Ambitious Teaching'. *Research in Drama Education Themed Issue: Teaching Shakespeare: Digital Processes*, 25(1), 143–46. https://doi.org /10.1080/13569783.2019.1687290.

Windschitl, M., J. Thompson, and M. Braaten (2011). 'Ambitious Pedagogy by Novice Teachers: Who Benefits from Tool-supported Collaborative Inquiry into Practice and Why?' *Teachers College Record*, 113(7), 1311–60.

To Pete and Reed, and every educator striving to teach ambitiously

Shakespeare and Pedagogy

Liam E. Semler
University of Sydney

Liam E. Semler is Professor of Early Modern Literature in the Department of English at the University of Sydney. He is author of *Teaching Shakespeare and Marlowe: Learning versus the System* (2013) and co-editor (with Kate Flaherty and Penny Gay) of *Teaching Shakespeare beyond the Centre: Australasian Perspectives* (2013). He is editor of *Coriolanus: A Critical Reader* (2021) and co-editor (with Claire Hansen and Jackie Manuel) of *Reimagining Shakespeare Education: Teaching and Learning through Collaboration* (Cambridge, forthcoming). His most recent book outside Shakespeare studies is *The Early Modern Grotesque: English Sources and Documents 1500–1700* (2019). Liam leads the Better Strangers project which hosts the open-access Shakespeare Reloaded website (shakespearereloaded.edu.au).

Gillian Woods
Birkbeck College, University of London

Gillian Woods is Reader in Renaissance Literature and Theatre at Birkbeck College, University of London. She is the author of *Shakespeare's Unreformed Fictions* (2013; joint winner of Shakespeare's Globe Book Award), *Romeo and Juliet: A Reader's Guide to Essential Criticism* (2012), and numerous articles about Renaissance drama. She is the co-editor (with Sarah Dustagheer) of *Stage Directions and Shakespearean Theatre* (2018). She is currently working on a new edition of *A Midsummer Night's Dream* for Cambridge University Press, as well as a Leverhulme-funded monograph about Renaissance Theatricalities. As founding director of the Shakespeare Teachers' Conversations, she runs a seminar series that brings together university academics, school teachers and educationalists from non-traditional sectors, and she regularly runs workshops for schools.

About the Series

The teaching and learning of Shakespeare around the world is complex and changing. *Elements in Shakespeare and Pedagogy* synthesises theory and practice, including provocative, original pieces of research, as well as dynamic, practical engagements with learning contexts.

Cambridge Elements ☰

Shakespeare and Pedagogy

ELEMENTS IN THE SERIES

Shakespeare and Virtual Reality
Edited by Stephen Wittek and David McInnis

Reading Shakespeare through Drama
Jane Coles and Maggie Pitfield

Podcasts and Feminist Shakespeare Pedagogy
Varsha Panjwani

Anti-Racist Shakespeare
Ambereen Dadabhoy and Nedda Mehdizadeh

Teaching Shakespeare and His Sisters
Emma Whipday

Shakespeare and Place-Based Learning
Claire Hansen

Teaching with Interactive Shakespeare Editions
Laura B. Turchi

A full series listing is available at: www.cambridge.org/ESPG

Printed in the United States
by Baker & Taylor Publisher Services